THE IMMIGRANT SURVIVAL GUIDE TO SILICON VALLEY

By: Carlos Quezada

Foreword

Written By Nasa Astronaut Dr. José Hernández

Copyright ©2024 Carlos Quezada. Publishing through Rising Above Publishing Services. All rights reserved.

No part of this book may be reproduced in any form or by any mechanical means, including information storage and retrieval systems without permission in writing from the publisher/author, except by a reviewer who may quote passages in a review.

The information shared in this book represents experiences lived through by the author. Any resemblance to actual persons, living or dead, or actual events is purely coincidental. The advice and strategies discussed may not be suitable for every situation.

Author: Carlos Quezada

Forword By: José Hernández

Contributors: Martha Niño Rodriguez, Yai Vargas, Rocío Pérez, Catalina Peña, Oscar Garcia, Jesse Cortez, and Dr. Johnny Thomas

ISBN: 9798320071022

> QUANTITY PURCHASES: Schools, companies, professional groups, clubs,

and other organizations may qualify for special terms when ordering quantities of this title.

Table of Contents

01 — Expanding Your Horizons — 18
Contribution By Martha Niño Rodriguez — *32*

02 — Finding A Coach, Mentor & Sponsor — 37
Contribution By Yai Vargas — *50*

03 — Elevate Yourself — 55
Contribution By Rocío Pérez — *69*

04 — Impossible Is Nothing — 76

05 — Be Bold — 85
Contribution By Catalina Peña — *95*

06 — Imposter Syndrome — 101
Contribution By Oscar Garcia — *110*

07 — Authentic Leadership — 117
Contribution By Jesse Cortez — *126*

08 — Keeping The Faith — 136
Contribution By Dr. Johnny Thomas — *139*

09 — The Generational Success Staircase — 145

About The Author — 152

DEDICATION

To my wife and children, your unwavering support and patience have been the cornerstone of my journey. you are my constant inspiration. To my parents, whose values, beliefs, grit, and tenacity have shaped the very foundation of who I am today – thank you for being my guiding stars.

To my siblings, fellow pioneers on our family's journey to success. Your resilience and shared ambition have been the wind beneath my wings.

This dedication extends to Tony Tavarez, a close family friend whose inspiration reverberates through generations, elevating not only my father but also my career trajectory.

Special acknowledgment to Ms. Miles, my high school teacher, for sparking my interest in computers and technology, laying the groundwork for a passion that became a lifelong pursuit.

Gratitude to Michael Pote, my first senior leader in tech, whose coaching and mentorship paved the way for my initial steps in this dynamic industry.

A heartfelt thank you to Jeff Abrew, a manager who saw potential in me and set a remarkable example of leading with empathy.

I'd also like to dedicate this book to Jorge Delgadillo, a former manager and lifelong friend, your role as my first and only Mexican manager in my career was transformative. Your inspirational leadership made me believe that Latinos could not only succeed but also excel in leadership positions.

To Miguel "Wilson" Cruz, for guiding me through uncharted waters and illuminating the path to success in the realm of international business. Your mentorship was the compass that steered me through unfamiliar territories, and your unwavering support ensured I never faltered. With each journey across Latin America, you instilled in me the wisdom and grace necessary to navigate any challenge that arose. Thank you for being more than a coach- a beacon of inspiration and a steadfast guide.

This book is also dedicated to all my pillars of support and sources of inspiration.

Y para mi gente!

JOSÉ HERNÁNDEZ

President and CEO of
Tierra Luna Engineering, LLC

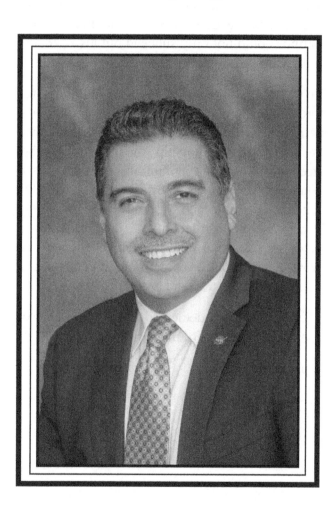

FOREWORD

I am thrilled to introduce you to a remarkable guide penned by an insightful author and dear friend, Carlos Quezada. In, "The Immigrant Survival Guide to Silicon Valley," Carlos masterfully weaves together the wisdom derived from personal experience along with the stories of other successful individuals who have conquered the dynamic landscape of Silicon Valley.

"Expanding Your Horizons," opens the door to a journey that transcends boundaries, encouraging you to dream beyond the ordinary. Carlos's ability to foster resilience, handle change, and thrive under pressure is at the heart of this guide, echoed in each chapter that follows.

The chapters, "Finding Your Mentor" and "Elevate Yourself" not only explore the vital role of mentorship but also delve into the art of networking, revealing the secrets of leveraging connections in the fast-paced world of Silicon Valley. In the chapter, "Impossible is Nothing," "Be Bold," and "Imposter Syndrome," Carlos fearlessly addresses the challenges many of us have and continue to face.

"Authentic Leadership" and the poignant subsection, "It's Not Just About You," illuminate the path to leadership with integrity and emphasize the interconnectedness of our journeys. Carlos brilliantly demonstrates how the immigrant spirit, characterized by the ability to handle change and thrive under pressure, is the ultimate survival gene in the high-tech environment. In "Keeping the Faith," Carlos takes us on a voyage through the unknown, drawing on the experiences of successful figures in the tech industry to illustrate the importance of tenacity as a superpower.

As a companion to my own book, "Reaching for the Stars," this guide goes beyond the theoretical, providing a tangible roadmap for success in Silicon Valley. The immigrant experience is an asset, and Carlos Quezada shows us how to harness its unique attributes to not just survive but flourish.

Silicon Valley, with its ever-changing landscape, demands adaptability and resilience, qualities inherently possessed by immigrants. Carlos Quezada's "The Immigrant Survival Guide to Silicon Valley" is a testament to the strength, perseverance, and innovation that define the immigrant journey, making it an indispensable resource for anyone navigating the complexities of the tech industry.

May this guide be your compass in the hustle and bustle of Silicon Valley, propelling you toward success and inspiring you to reach new heights.

Warm regards,

Astronaut José M. Hernández

PROLOGUE

As I reflect and learn to embrace the blessings bestowed upon me, it's truly astonishing to consider the life I lead. Receiving compliments has never been my forte. Before stepping onto the stage for a keynote, joining a panel, or facilitating a mentorship session, I often question why people would be interested in hearing from me. Who am I to share insights? I've yet to fully comprehend or acknowledge that my journey is perceived as unique. In my eyes, it's just a personal narrative, neither distinct nor extraordinary—simply my own.

You see, I'm just the son of a migrant farm worker and very ambitious mother. My mom was the first entrepreneur in my life. Understandably, my path to where I am today has been very unconventional and non-traditional. As I continue to share my story with others, I realize my story resonates with many of those in the immigrant community and is not that unique at all.

The art of the hustle has always been the brush that I've used to paint the story of my life. I've never known any other way. I was born in the small farming community of Degollado, Jalisco Mexico. A town where everyone knows each other. In my early childhood while my mother and I lived in Mexico, my father was picking fruits and vegetables in the fields of Salinas, Modesto, and Santa Barbara, California. I first came to the United States at the young age of two years old. Even though I was much too young to remember, the following twelve years consisted of one to two-year cycles of continuous uprooting where we would move between Mexico and the United States. I am reminded of Astronaut Dr. Jose Hernández sharing a similar story during his upbringing while being raised in the fields of the California Central Valley. One of his comments that really resonated with me is, when you constantly move around like that you never have the opportunity to grow roots and establish yourself.

In retrospect, I truly value the opportunity I had to be raised in a multicultural environment. I went from living on a farm to living in the city, from attending school where Spanish was spoken to transitioning to an English-speaking school. I went from being surrounded by familiar faces at school to suddenly finding myself at Silver Creek High School in San Jose, where there were nearly 2,000 students and I didn't know anyone.

It is experiencing continuous change and constantly adapting to my surroundings that have made me who I am today. This was also helpful in my career at startup companies. One thing you also must be great at when working for startups in Silicon Valley, is adjusting to change, being quick on your feet, and having the ability to pivot when necessary. Interestingly, these are qualities that many immigrants, regardless of their country of origin, tend to possess. It is crucial for us to understand how to utilize and capitalize on these attributes to propel ourselves forward.

It was the summer before my senior year of high school when I was thirteen years old that I had finally obtained permanent legal status in the United States. By this point, my sister and I had developed a strong command of the English language after years of participating in ESL (English as a Second Language) programs. In our immediate family, no one had graduated from high school, so obtaining a high school diploma was seen as the pinnacle of success for my sister and me. At that time, neither our parents nor I understood the significance of a GPA; all we knew was that we needed to graduate. However, I soon discovered that graduating was more challenging than I had anticipated. Failing the second semester of government during my senior year prevented me from graduating with my class and participating in the graduation ceremony. Instead, I had to take summer school classes to complete my high school education, and I received my diploma from the front office, devoid of any ceremonial experience.

It was a moment that I never expected would have such a profound impact on my life. You see, as first-generation immigrants, my parents took on the role of providers and survivors. Their goal was to create a better life for their children, and their sacrifices were meant to pave the way for our success. Like many first-generation parents, they saw graduating high school as a measure of their own success, a way to prove that their hard work and sacrifices were worthwhile. I will never forget the disappointment in my father's eyes when I told him I wouldn't be graduating and walking the stage with my classmates. That look, more than 20 years ago, still drives me today. I realized that I was a product of all the sacrifices and hard work my parents had endured. I understood the responsibility I had to fulfill their dreams. I needed to show them that their sacrifices were not in vain. In that moment, with tears in my eyes, I made a promise to my parents that I would make it up to them. Even though they didn't get to see me walk the stage in high school, I knew I had to go back to school and pursue a higher level of education so that I could give them the experience of seeing me graduate and walk the stage.

Sometimes I wonder if I had graduated from high school on time, would I have continued my education? Afterall, I would have achieved my parents' expectation of me and not had the pressure to continue my education. Honestly, had I graduated, I don't think I would have had the motivation to further my education because not only was my high school GPA horrible, but I had never planned to go to school after high school. I had no clue on how to even pursue going to a traditional college. Thankfully, that's not how it turned out. I saw a TV commercial of a trade school while sitting home around lunch time watching an episode of Maury Povich (I chuckle thinking about all the time I listed to Maury say, "You are not the father."). The trade school bragged about their computer program, and I was inspired. You see, when I would get asked, what I would do after high school, not having a clue I would reply, "I'm going to get into computers." Even though I had no clue what that meant, it was still enough to get people to feel proud of me and change the subject or go away. I enrolled in that trade school and after thirteen months, I was finally able to give my parents the graduation they had asked for. I graduated with an Associate in Science degree in Systems Administration and Networking from "Master's Institute of Technology." (Yes M.I.T). It was one of the proudest moments in my life. Having my parents in the audience as they announced my name while I headed for the stage and received my diploma is something I will never forget.

Riding the high of graduation, I realized that I really enjoyed learning about technology, I re-enrolled and got my Bachelor of Science in Computer Science. My running joke is I now have a B.S. from M.I.T. At the time, I felt I had made it. I had made it further than anyone in my family from an educational perspective. Little did I know the one thing that made me feel successful would be something that would act as a dark cloud over me for the early part of my career. Having a B.S. Degree from a school no one has heard of before is only impressive around those that don't know any better. Once you enter the workforce and are surrounded by folks who have a bachelor's or master's degrees from Stanford, Berkeley, Harvard, Yale, and all the other prestigious universities, you can't help but get kicked in the face by the imposter syndrome monster. Throughout the early part of my career, I constantly felt the need to hide where I went to school. I had always assumed that others knew more than me because I didn't graduate from a "prestigious" school. This belief became a heavy burden that I carried for over ten years in my career. However, I always knew I had something very valuable that I bring to the table: hustle, grit, and experience.

You see, while most of the folks with fancy degrees were busy studying at IVY league universities, I was hustling and working. Today, I joke and say, while others read books, I was writing them. This meant I had real world experience and perspectives they only read about. I had years of customer service, assembly line, and even public speaking experience through my various odd jobs. I was a butcher at a Mexican grocery store, worked my way up at a machine shop, motile notary, and even opened my own DJ business doing weddings, quinceañera, and EDM DJ at local clubs. This is where I felt I had a one up on most folks. It is this experience that I always leaned on to defeat the imposter syndrome monster. I had transferable skills that were now relevant in my current roles. I never had a problem speaking to customers or problem solving.

Imposter syndrome is a battle that I've had to deal with throughout my career, worrying about being too authentic and "taking off the mask," afraid of asking a stupid question, and dealing with cultural beliefs that we should just be grateful to have a job and not speak up and rock the boat. To have faith that our work will speak for itself, and that recognition and success will come on its own. This could not be further from the truth. I do not agree with "bringing your whole self to work." While I believe in bringing your culture and authenticity, we need to leave behind some of the cultural baggage which contributes to our servant and submissive mentality. We need to stop "being grateful for the opportunity."

I have made it a priority to take a non-conventional approach in my career and have not reached my current position by staying silent and waiting for others to acknowledge my work. However, I have always kept in mind the valuable lessons and education that my parents instilled in me. I do it with respect and from the heart.

As a Latino immigrant in America, I have learned that success can often be misunderstood. Throughout my journey, I have come to realize the significance of sharing the knowledge I have gained on how to succeed in life through sheer determination and the pure art of hustle. I feel truly blessed to have had the opportunities I have had and feel it's my responsibility to represent those who are afraid to speak up. It's my responsibility to bring others with me as I grow.

In this book, I want to share not only my experiences but have asked people in my life who have also touched me to share their experiences. My hope is the more we share our stories, the more someone out there can relate by seeing themselves in us. Our stories may be unique to each other, but they are not different. It is my passion in life to continually motivate, educate, and participate.

CHAPTER 1

EXPANDING YOUR HORIZONS

"You cannot dream of something which you do not know exists."

-Carlos Quezada

Growing up in the U.S., I've come to realize something interesting about my family life. We never left our "Honeycomb." You see, just like bees, we create this honeycomb of comfort, and we may leave it here and there, but we never go very far from it. Work, school, church, and our relatives all typically were within a five to ten square mile radius, and this small area is what I call our honeycomb.

When I was about five years old, we lived in a small immigrant community in Milpitas, California. It literally was a u-shaped cul-de-sac where many of the families that lived there were also from Degollado, Jalisco. I see this consistently in the immigrant communities. We surround ourselves with family and friends and form a community of support who understands our current situation. The honeycomb reference is because we're comfortable living isolated inside our comfort zone. In our case, everything we needed was inside our honeycomb like all the other families around us: work, school, church, and even the flea market, (which was an after-church Sunday ritual for many of us). We rarely left our ten-mile honeycomb. It felt safe, we were always surrounded by an environment that was comfortable and familiar. Unfortunately, this also meant we were also not surrounded by people who had succeeded in outgrowing the environment. Our honeycomb community was made up of blue-collar workers who shared similar goals and dreams- the American dream. The problem is we were all starting at zero. We didn't have anyone in our honeycomb who could guide us. We were all figuring it out as we went along. We had to work twice as hard to achieve similar results. The only way the honeycomb succeeds is by growing it. I feel it's super important to expand your horizons and leave your honeycomb, interact, and learn from people who have outgrown the honeycomb and have achieved great things. It is important to surround yourself with people who you are constantly learning from. There are multiple examples of this. Show me who you surround yourself with and I will tell you who you are. Or as I always say, if you find yourself in a room with a group of people, and you are the smartest person in that room, it's time to find a new room.

We cannot expect to grow if we do not expand our horizons and push ourselves outside of our comfort zone. It is when we live on the edge of the comfort zone that learning, growth, and opportunity begin. Pushing yourself outside of your comfort zone will naturally introduce you to new ideas, behaviors, people, and environments and as a result continue to expand your horizons. To dream big, you need to continue to expand your horizons and keep growing. I have always said, "You cannot dream of something you do not know exists."

As immigrants, when we first come to the United States, we are full of dreams, goals, and ambitions. However, the struggle can quickly beat us down into complacency. It is imperative that we do not allow ourselves to fall into complacency. It is easy to get consumed with the monotony of the daily routines and forget what motivated us in the first place. First-gen immigrants can quickly become victims of their circumstances and concede to accept they may not be deserving of more and put the burden on their children to strive for greatness. It's very easy to lose your drive, your hunger, your ambition, and focus, and fall into this redundant cycle of complacency.

Whatever your circumstance may be, you cannot expect to break these generational cycles unless we change the narrative.

Here are some ways you can consider in order to expand your horizons:

Find a new routine: We are creatures of habit. While positive habits and daily rituals are great, being attached to only one way of doing them can keep us stuck and attribute towards a rigid way of thinking that blocks our minds from expanding. Whether you drive, hitch a ride or take public transportation, we tend to not change our day-to-day routine. Make it a point to drive through a different part of town. Pick up coffee or pastries at a new spot you've never been to before. Get to know the people that work and shop there. You may find a new favorite restaurant or coffee shop or find a park you never knew existed. For me, it meant going to the side of town where the "rich" people lived. When you're an immigrant sometimes you feel like you're not worthy or don't belong in some of the more affluent areas. I refused to accept that narrative and made it a point to explore these areas and feel comfortable being present. This helped me better understand what I wanted for my family and myself.

Learn a new skill: Growing up the way I was raised, it was not uncommon for me to be familiar with general construction or blue-collar work. However, this would not expose me to alternate outcomes. It was when I took a liking to computers and started taking computer courses, that I got a better understanding of technology and began to surround myself with others who were also in technology. Get into photography, hiking, yoga, it doesn't matter. The point is, break the cycle and take the time to connect with others.

Connect: Nowadays with the internet and soon the metaverse, there is no limit to the opportunities to connect with like-minded individuals. With twitter groups and discord channels it's very easy to immerse yourself and connect with individuals who are willing to share their knowledge in a million different topics. The best part is language or accents are no longer a barrier to entry in these communities. In tech especially, with the ongoing push to drive Diversity, Equity and Inclusion there has never been a better time to connect, be yourself and bring your perspective.

Discover: Do something outside of the norm or outside of your comfort zone. For me, it was scuba diving. I had always been fascinated by it; however, I had never known anyone who had done it before. I literally went to a dive shop and signed up for classes. I was immediately surrounded by folks with shared interests who have since become lifelong friends. And now, I had a Mexican flag stitched into my dive gear. I want people to know the day they dived with me, they dived with a Mexican. It's very normal for me to be the only Mexican on the dive. It's up to us to change that. We need to show up where our people are not common. It's up to us to change what a "typical Hispanic" looks like.

Plan your next adventure: This is the literal part of broadening your horizon. Go somewhere you felt seemed distant or unreachable. For some of us, it's typical that we want to travel back to our native country when possible. It's somewhere that is familiar and brings comfort. But why not every other year pick a destination where you maybe don't speak the language. Or where you will experience a different culture all together. It is these experiences that help us better understand each other and experiences you will be able to share at a later date in a networking environment. This, believe it or not, can also help break imposter syndrome in certain settings. We'll discuss this later.

Warning! As you work to grow yourself, one of the natural phenomena that will occur is you will begin to shed part of your community. You will quickly realize there are people in your community that either do not add any value or are preventing you from growing. Most immigrants are very family oriented and weigh the family's opinion very heavily. Many times, it is our own family who are the biggest crusher of dreams with comments like, "That's not for people like us," or, "You don't have the right level of education for that," or the infamous, "Look at you. You think you're all that now because of BLAH…BLAH."

One thing I have learned is that even though you will absolutely shed people from your community, you will form new communities as you continue to grow, I always say, if you want to grow, look at the folks you surround yourself with. If you were all in a room, would you be the smartest person in the room? If so, it's time to find another room. You see, when you are the smartest person in the room, you are no longer learning or growing. You are carrying the other folks in the room and many times unable to grow as you are constantly trying to grow them. This is something I am very guilty of, always looking to grow others and forget to continue to grow myself. It's important to always surround yourself with folks who will add value to you too.

The law of attraction is something I have always felt very strongly about. First, what is the law of attraction? The technical definition is:

"The <u>law of attraction</u> is a philosophy suggesting that positive thoughts bring positive results into a person's life, while negative thoughts bring negative outcomes. It is based on the belief that thoughts are a form of energy and that positive energy attracts success in all areas of life, including health, finances, and relationships."

For me, the law of attraction is about publicly and continuously manifesting and sharing what your wishes, hopes, and goals are. Let the universe, God, or whatever you believe in take care of the rest. It's the concept of sharing what your goals and aspirations are out loud in the right forum. I say the right forum because you must be very careful. As mentioned previously, sharing your goals and aspirations amongst family may sometimes result in negative feedback that you were not looking for. Family and friends who feel comfortable around you may quickly tell you why you can't do something, and that is partially because they can't add any value to help you accomplish those dreams or aspirations. However, in the right circles, you may share your dreams and aspirations and more often than not you will find that there will be someone who may have the expertise, education, or network to help you get closer to that dream.

I do this a lot in professional settings. For example: imagine yourself at a networking event. You're in a circle of about seven to ten people holding a cocktail talking about what you do for work, or where you are from. The level of experience in the group varies from early career to senior level people. It's a very causal setting. Then you say, "You know what I've always wanted to do…." and that's your moment. Naturally people will want to give you advice or connect you with someone. This happens to me all the time. The more you do this, you will realize the opportunities are out there. You don't have to do it alone, and just like that, you expanded your circle, your community, and your horizons. Your honeycomb just grew.

When you first come to the United States as an immigrant you feel so helpless. There are so many challenges and decisions to be made. Immigrants are problem solvers. How do we solve problems? We normally start small. As immigrants we all share the "Survival Gene." We immediately start breaking down problems into smaller pieces and get to work.

Some of the initial decisions to be made are: Where are we going to live? How will I make money to eat or feed our family? It is not until later that we can consider any type of comforts or luxuries. Initially, we are eager to quickly start working and earning money so we can improve the situation we left behind back in our home country. Unfortunately, we run the risk of focusing on continuing to earn survival rate money that sometimes we become complacent. If we make enough to put a roof over our heads, food in the fridge, and possibly send what's left over back to our home country, we sometimes feel we have made it.

But why not think bigger? As first-generation immigrants are we really damned to accept the fact that we may not have the legal documentation to work here? Or do we really believe that we may not be able to grow beyond blue-collar work due to our education? These are all limits that are self -imposed. When we all left our country, we were extremely motivated and driven for better.

However, we are quickly beaten down by the live to work routine that we are often faced with just to survive. How can you possibly find the time to go to school, learn a new skill or learn how to grow when you're already working two jobs while supporting your family here and back in your home country?

It's important to never forget why you came to the United States. What motivated you or your family to come here? What were the dreams of you or your parents when the sacrifice to leave everything behind was made. This is the fire in the belly of the immigrants that makes us tenacious, full of grit, and an overwhelming desire to survive. We do not give up. However, how do we break the monotony of the immigrant work/life schedule? We need to strive for more. Yet, how do we achieve more? Expand your horizons.

When I graduated high school, I did not know of anyone who had attended college. I didn't understand what the requirements were, the need for an SAT test etc. I was expected to take the English and basic skills that I learned in high school and find a job that paid a decent hourly wage so that I could start contributing back to the household. Back in those days, minimum wage was around $4.25/hr. For obvious reasons, it would have been a huge deal if I could find a job that paid $8-10 an hour. Alternatively, I could go look for a job at a construction company and get into manual labor. Because I spoke decent English there may have been an opportunity to quickly rise through the ranks and get into a lead or supervisory position quickly as I would be able to translate between the rest of the workers and the customers.

But what changed? Why did I not fall into the pre-defined stereo type?

Step 1. Broaden your horizons. Think bigger. "You can only dream that which you have seen or experienced" Example of dream car, dream house, relationship, career....

Step 2. Persist and don't give up. Our failures are only lessons of what to do and what not to do. Use your small achievements as motivation to keep going and to do more. Don't stop challenging yourself and learning tools on how to expand your mindset.

Step 3. Seek and or create opportunities to surround yourself with people that you normally wouldn't be around, particularly high achievers, and immerse yourself in different experiences. Through these experiences you can create authentic connections that can lead to mentorship as well as opportunities.

Step 4. Speak up. Don't shy away from telling the RIGHT people your accomplishments and even more importantly, your ambitions and needs.

Step 5. Lean into your faith as you make room for new in your life. Change can be difficult and uncomfortable, but it is necessary to create a different type of life than what is around you. If people leave your life, let them. The right people will stay. If you become aware of a self-sabotaging way of thinking or behavior, let it go. Allow yourself to be open to shedding everything that doesn't align with the future life that you are creating.

REFLECTION QUESTION:

What ways do you manifest in your life and how have they been working for you? If you don't have any, research (Google), and list below some manifestation techniques that you can start doing.

MARTHA NIÑO RODRIGUEZ

Silicon Valley Professional-25+ years | Speaker | Author | Foundation Founder - Immigrant.

THE BEAUTY OF SAFE

By: Martha Niño Rodriguez

I was the kid in school that was terrified of recess because I'd get beat up. I had red hair and was picked on. I was from Mexico, poor, and was called nasty names. I was always in the free lunch line. I never fought back. I would just put my head down and take it.

I was born in a shack with no water, no electricity in a small town called Pueblo Viejo in Mexico. I had no crib. My mother converted an old dresser drawer she had found into my crib. Although this was not conventional, it kept me safe. That was the start to my life. Later in life we had made the journey to the U.S. undocumented, and I left the dresser drawer behind and slept in a one- bedroom home with eight other people. Although our situation was not conventional, I was safe, and now we had water and electricity - better was happening. As I became a teen, I was craving space, my parents moved out the washing machine from the laundry room and cut a twin mattress about a half foot just so it could fit into the small space - that laundry room became my first bedroom and the first time I had space of my own. My mom was resourceful and creative, and used to turn bed sheets into curtains, and although I only had an old converted bedsheet as my curtain separating me from the rest of the household. I felt safe in my unconventional bedroom. Sometimes all you need to create opportunity is resourcefulness and imagination. With help from mom and dad I had maximized an opportunity. With every change there was a craving for better. Keep in mind, better is so different for everyone, and being poor in a third world country is so different than being poor in the U.S. Life is about perspectives, and it's our perspective that shapes our reality and our idea of what success is. For me at that time, that laundry room in the U.S. made me feel rich! That feeling motivated me to look and create more opportunities for myself despite what the outside world may have thought about me or my family.

We rarely went to malls or real grocery stores. With my parents earning minimum wages, my mother became the most efficient shopper I knew, and she still is. She knew where all the sales were and when. For clothes we went to the Goodwill. For food she made everything out of what others would think is nothing, and with just a few dollars somehow mom made feasts. Across the street from one of those Goodwill store was an old Wonder Bread store. The items sold there were slightly wonky, a little older, perhaps didn't sell in the conventional stores. The store had cement floors and the lighting was dim, but we didn't care. It was our opportunity to perhaps get a pastry at half price, even if the date or packaging were a little off.

Who makes up this stuff, and gets to say that something is off anyways? Who decides dates? Who decides imperfect looking muffins are not delicious. To us they were fine. OFF worked for us - they were actually PERFECT.

When society or someone tells us we are NOT, it is important for us to remember who made those rules up. Really analyze who is saying you can't or aren't – sometimes, things might merely be a suggestion, you might be perfect for those that actually need you most.

I remember biting into a pastry from an expired crooked, dented package - it was heaven. That bread was not old, it was resilient - it made it through stuff and there it was ready to for a family to feast, this bread was needed - it just needed to be looked at a little different. My parents didn't have much but they made it work. My mother continues to shop in the clearance section of stores, dollar outlets and those Goodwill stores which were once so shameful, but have now become trendy. Don't take for granted memories of little things, the smells, the feeling - remembering is a gift and those little things may actually be some of the biggest things in our lives, because it reminds us of how it felt to be grateful. It is through the lens of gratitude that allows us to lift our head up and look around, and see opportunity where others may see walls. Only through this lens can we limitlessly create using our lives as the canvas, and our imagination as the brush.

As I look at pictures of this little girl, I get sad. Many people took advantage of her. Today, I want to tell her that all of that will stop one day, that she will have the courage to stop the bullies. She will fight back, and she will speak not only for her, but for others and that they will feel hope because of her story. I would also remind her that yes, it will require hard work. Yes, it will be uncomfortable at times, and yes she will fall but she'll also dust herself right off and get back up even stronger than before That all of this will happen the day that she decides to lift her head up to see past her horizon, and when she does, she will be so proud.

CHAPTER 2

FINDING A COACH, MENTOR & SPONSOR

Most immigrants, graduates, and early career individuals don't have it figured out, and really don't know what they want to do with the rest of their lives. That's expected. I know I sure didn't. What I do know is that I not only stayed open to the possibilities, but I also remained curious. The unknown can be scary for many. Knowing what to expect next gives us some sort of comfort that allows us to prepare exactly for what we know is coming, giving nothing more and nothing less. Although there is nothing wrong with this way of living, it is not where dreams of breaking the mold of mediocrity live. You must stay curious and be open to explore unknown terrain and learn to be ok with being uncomfortable, because change lies at the edge of our comfort zones. Having someone to help you navigate through is key. The following story is how this concept changed the course of my life forever.

During the late seventies my father worked as a commercial landscaper in what would later become known as "Silicon Valley." He worked in setting up irrigation systems, mowing lawns, and trimming trees in companies we would later recognize as tech giants. He referred to them as "Electrónicas." After many years working in landscaping, Tony, a good friend of his questioned him on how much longer he'd be in landscaping. My father knew that he could work hard but didn't think that he was entitled to anything other than blue collar jobs. Tony, however, believed in my father and felt that he had the potential to do so much more. At the time, Tony was working inside one of these electrónicas and encouraged my father to apply.

After reluctantly submitting the application, my father ended up landing an interview. My father was under the impression he was interviewing for a permanent landscaping position at the company. During the interview my father was asked if you ever worked at an electronics company. My father responded excitedly, "Yes, of course," and he started to name off a few, "You know like Atari, Comag, IBM." My father showed up to the interview wearing construction boots and jeans which still had remnants of pipe glue and a long sleeve shirt. Although my father was not dressed to impress during the interview, he still managed to impress them enough because of what they interpreted as his work history at all those companies. A few days later he was offered the job. His first day on the job, my father showed up wearing the same work outfit. Upon checking in for his first day he was quickly given a white lab coat and anti static bracelet and escorted over to his workbench where he was expected to work, bench testing microchips. My father was puzzled. He had never touched any of the equipment in front of him. He asked about the workbench, and about the tools on the workbench. He had no idea how to use any of them. He went to his manager for clarification. Where was the shovel or the tool shack? His manager seemed puzzled and asked, "What do you mean, haven't you done this before? What did you do at Comag, Atari and IBM." My father smiled and responded, "I did the landscaping, replaced sprinklers, fixed broken pipes, and trimmed trees." I'm convinced that the manager was too embarrassed to admit that he did not do a good job of interviewing my father. The manager went back to Tony who had recommended him. Tony explained he had recommended him for an entry level job and felt he was a fast learner and could be trained. They moved my father off the bench and put him marking and packing parts. My dad was grateful for the opportunity because he knew that he had a job rain or shine.

How did my dad end up working at a high-tech company? Because Tony knew my dad's character, his work ethic and he believed in him. (This is an example of a sponsor) Over the course of 23 years, my dad held several rolls at the company. Tony was always there to coach and encourage him to overcome what we now know as imposter syndrome. He helped my father believe in himself and that he deserved to be there. He'd also constantly check up on him, give him advice, and push him to not only do more but to stand up for himself too. During my father's time at the company, he received a lot of recognition for the work that he was doing and was continually promoted. After over 20 years at the company my father eventually became a people leader where he led the Quality Assurance test floor. He went from marking and packing parts to leading the QA production team for North America. He traveled to Boston and Taiwan to showcase his team's work at a global level. After 23 years at the company, my father finally retired as a global QA manager for the test fLoor. Pretty impressive for a person who joined the company thinking he was fixing broken sprinkler pipes and trimming trees. Had it not been for the ongoing coaching and mentorship that he had from Tony my father may not have continued to grow within the company. Tony was my father's coach, mentor, and sponsor.

Everyone Needs a Tony

Tony didn't only help my father but was instrumental in my life. When I was in high school, he would come over to the house around tax season to help my father with his taxes. He was the only person I ever met that had a laptop. During that time, computers in the home were very rare. I still remember the size of that Toshiba Satellite Pro laptop running TurboTax- that thing was huge. When he would come over, I was always very curious about the laptop. I would peek around his shoulder to try to get a glimpse of what he was doing. Rather than being overly cautious about his laptop, once Tony was done with the taxes, he and my dad would go in the backyard and have a beer. While he was hanging out with my father, Tony would allow me to use his laptop and play some games. It was then that he would encourage me to consider a career in computers. He told me that computers were the future and that there was good money in computers. A few years ago, I was on a panel, and I was asked who in my life had influenced me to pursue a career in tech. It was at that moment, on that panel that I realized that I had not really thought about it. How did I end up here? Over the past 20 years I spent my entire career in tech. I'm a network engineer by education and a wireless architect and RF engineer by trade. I have a background in Machine Learning / AI and Big Data analytics. I spent the first couple of years of my career traveling across Latin America. I lived and breathed computers and technology. Yet, as I sit on this panel, I didn't have a good answer. After some reflection it hit me. It was Tony. Not only had he impacted my father's life but had also influenced mine tremendously.

As I mentioned earlier, I wasn't a very good student in high school. My senior year I was not able to walk the stage with my classmates. My father at the time was a people leader of the company and I can remember him telling me that many of his employees had been taking days off to attend their children's graduation. My father came and asked, "Mijo, when is your graduation day? I want to make sure that I take the day off so I can come see you walk the stage." I could not look him in the eyes, instead I looked at the floor and explained that I messed up and admitted that I would not be walking the stage or graduating with my class. The look of disappointment in my father's eyes is something that I will never forget. I felt horrible. It impacted me so much that I remember apologizing profusely and promising that I would make it up to him. Later, when Tony asked me, "Carlos what are your plans after high school?" The best answer I could give him was, "I want to study computers." I knew that would impress Tony and my father. So, I promised my father I was going to study computers after high school and that he would finally see me graduate. At that point I had no idea what that meant but I knew if my father taught me anything, it was that a man is nothing without his word. I ended up inviting Tony to my A.S and B.S graduation ceremony. At the time, 20 years later, I was a Senior Director role of a company who is recognized as the "Birthplace of Silicon Valley," Hewlett-Packard, (HP). Although throughout my career I did more than work with computers. I enabled towns/villages and cities to have access to the internet for the first time ever. I've helped design networks for stadiums, hospitals, hotels etc. I've held various leadership roles managing hundreds of people. However, my parents have no clue what I do. To them I work with computers. After realizing how influential Tony had been to my career decision and the path my life had taken, I felt like he was one of the few people that could truly understand my career journey. I decided to reach out to Tony on LinkedIn. I wanted to thank him for the influence that he had not only in my father's life, but also in mine. I wanted him to know how influential those conversations over my dad's W-2s really were. I felt like he could appreciate the gravity of what I had accomplished. Considering that I didn't go to university but a small trade school and still had managed to excel in my career. I wanted to thank him in person for what he had done for both my father and me. We messaged back-and-forth on LinkedIn. I remember it like it was yesterday. It was a Thursday afternoon and we had agreed that we were going to have lunch the following Tuesday. I had looked for a restaurant that was close to both of us. My plan was to meet him and hand him my business card and officially introduce myself to him as a Senior Director Global Services. I wanted him to feel proud but also fulfilled for what he had done for not only me and my father's lives, but also my children's lives as well. I would now be able to carry it forward and raise the bar for my kids. All thanks for the conversation he had with me during tax season. Unfortunately, as I write this today, I am overcome with sadness. Sadly, I was not able to have a conversation with Tony. The last message I exchanged with him was on that Thursday, and the following Sunday Tony passed away. I never had the opportunity to look Tony in the eyes and say thanks. I was never able to tell him thanks for sparking what would eventually become a huge flame that motivates and drives me. I'll never forget the impact that he had on my life and since I cannot say thanks to him, at least I can honor him by carrying the torch he lit. The story of Tony and my father is also one of the reasons why I feel it's my responsibility to be somebody else's Tony. I now understand the responsibility that I have as a Hispanic leader in tech to help push up and pull up other Latinos, and to give people the same opportunity that my dad was given.

People may not always have all the experience on their resume. However, one trait all immigrants share is desire to survive and thrive. There is an inherit work ethic in the immigrant community and I want to help people recognize their full potential and give them the coaching and opportunities to succeed so they themselves can also succeed and have a better tomorrow for their family.

WHAT IS THE DIFFERENCE BETWEEN A COACH, MENTOR, & SPONSOR?

Coach: Like in sports, a coach is someone that speaks at you. They can give you immediate feedback while you're doing something to change your behavior. Essentially, they speak to you live.

Mentor: A mentor speaks with you. The mentor understands you, understands what you are trying to do. They may have done it before and give you feedback on how to do things differently or bring a different perspective for you to try next time you are "doing the thing".

Sponsor: A sponsor is someone who speaks about you when you're not in the room. A sponsor is not something you ask for. It's something you earn. Someone who has seen you or your work and believes in you. Someone who knows what you're working on and where you're going. They are the ones who will recommend you in a meeting that you're not even in. Many times, you may not even know they are a sponsor. Sponsorship will happen organically as part of good work ethic, making sure that you are celebrating your work and build a good personal brand.

You may be wondering how you can find a coach or mentor. I call it, "Find your Rabbit." The rabbit reference comes from dog races (Saw it on a bugs bunny cartoon once). You see, in dog races what inspires the dogs to run and run fast is a mechanical rabbit they chase down the track. In this case, your rabbit is someone who's already been there and done that. Someone who already has the job or role you'd like to have someday. My suggestion is to pick one thing you want to do, and then find someone that is not only doing it but succeeding at it. In this world, it's not necessarily what you know, it's who you know, and relationships are key to success. A mentorship is a two-way relationship that requires, just like any other relationship, reciprocity, and time.

Going into it with 'what can I get out of this' type of attitude will not lead you anywhere, because ultimately you should be seeking a mentorship relationship with a person that you would want around you for the long haul; someone you can connect and vibe with. You don't want it to feel like an obligation to be around this person. Therefore, carefully select who you want your rabbit to be.

After, put yourself out there and ask them out for coffee or lunch to get to know them more and vice versa. Although, it may sound corny, asking the person to be your mentor is probably the way to go so that there is clarity on the relationship. Most people are willing to help others that genuinely want to learn and are willing to put the work in. When you reach a certain threshold in your career and expertise, guaranteed, you've learned many valuable lessons that took years to learn. Being able to save someone years from learning the same lesson is very fulfilling and you'd be surprised how many will take their mentorship role in your life very seriously. And remember, as you grow, you can always be someone's rabbit!

I'd like to officially say thank you to Tony and his family! Thank you for helping my father realize his full potential. Thank you for inspiring me to push for better and for the opportunity to learn from your leadership which has enabled me to pass this on to my family and others. Everybody needs a Tony, and I hope that one day I can live up to be somebody's Tony.

REFLECTION QUESTION:

Who is or can potentially be your Tony? Brainstorm here some goals or careers that you want to attain or accomplish and research some people in your community that could possibly fit the role of your mentor.

YAI VARGAS

Vice President, Strategic Engagements
Hispanic Association on Corporate Responsibility

FINDING A MENTOR

By: Yai Vargas

As an immigrant from the Dominican Republic who didn't have parents that grew up here, no less in corporate America, it was difficult to navigate the importance of finding mentors and sponsors to guide my career journey. It wasn't until I started having conversations with one of my first managers in a corporate setting that I realized I was incredibly unprepared to make decisions that would eventually lead to a "successful" and impactful career

Think of your situation right now, your role, responsibilities, your salary, your bonus, your relationship to your manager, your direct reports - everything. Can you attribute your good or bad career decisions to the knowledge you have acquired at school, through conversations, your friends or parents? Perhaps you are one who indeed has a mentor or sponsor who has helped break down aspects of all these career decisions and helped you take those very calculated steps.

Finding a mentor as a Latina professional can be crucial for various reasons, and the choice of mentors, whether they share your background or are different, can offer unique benefits.

Here are some areas of focus I look for when it comes to identifying the right mentor:

Representation & Relatability.

A mentor who shares a similar cultural background, such as being Latina, can provide a sense of representation - someone who can really understand why it's not in our culture to talk back to a manager or knows why I've never been taught to talk about money or ask for a raise or promotion. This mentor may have faced similar challenges and can offer insights into navigating the workplace as a Latina professional.

On the other hand, having mentors from different backgrounds can expose you to diverse perspectives and approaches. Connecting and learning from a mentor who isn't Latina can enrich my understanding of various work environments, connections and broaden my professional horizons.

Networking Opportunities:

I can't tell you how many times I have connected with a Latina who has offered to help me find a job, access events and even refer clients to me when I was an entrepreneur. There is this natural immediate beautiful bond when you meet a Latina who really has your back. A mentor who shares your cultural background may have a network that includes individuals from similar backgrounds, providing valuable networking opportunities within your community.

Mentors from different backgrounds can introduce you to a more diverse network, helping you connect with professionals from various industries and backgrounds.

Cultural Intelligence:

I speak about this topic a lot. Having a mentor who understands your cultural context can help you navigate cultural nuances in the workplace, enhancing the way you do business with diversity and traditions, values, and intersectional ties in the forefront. I honestly enjoy having diverse perspectives and exposure to mentors with different backgrounds which can also enhance your ability to work effectively in diverse teams and across various cultural contexts. The more you learn about how others communicate, engage, lead and empower others, the more you become a human-centered leader in your journey.

Ultimately, the key is to curate and strike a balance for your unique career needs - and that can (and should) change over time. Having mentors who share your background can provide a strong support system, while mentors from diverse backgrounds can contribute to a more comprehensive and inclusive professional development journey. It's essential to be open to learning from a variety of mentors and leveraging the strengths that each mentorship dynamic offers. My hope for you is that you realize that you're also capable of teaching, mentoring, leading, and sponsoring others, just like you have received.

If you're reading this, it's time you reflect on what the most impactful advice you've received is and who you can share that with now to make a difference in your career journey.

CHAPTER 3

ELEVATE YOURSELF

"Success is never linear. Everybody's staircase to success is different."

Carlos Quezada

If you'd ask my parents what I do for a living, they probably couldn't tell you. They are very supportive and proud of my accomplishments but couldn't tell you what I do. I think they still think I fix computers. Unfortunately, in some cases people will find that their biggest supporters are not always their families and friends. Some of the closest people around may say things like, "That's not for people like us" or "Don't get your hopes up, that's only for rich people," or, "School isn't for you. Who are you kidding? You need to work." It's just the way things are, but unfortunately many people allow this to stop them from growing and continuing to develop themselves. Finding your 'tribe', your outside support group is key to really growing for everyone. We all need people in our corner who believe in our capabilities and see us for who we are in the present time, not where we came from or who we once were. People can only see you through the lenses of their own limits, so being intentional about surrounding yourself with people that have unlimited mindsets is really the key.

Power of Association

When people from other countries come to the U.S., whether legally or illegally, we all share a common trait: ambition, motivation, drive, and hunger. This hunger becomes our fuel. However, in most cases, we start losing momentum. One reason for this is surrounding ourselves with people who have low aspirations. They praise us and make us feel like we've achieved a lot and that we've made it, but their standards are low. We may be made to believe we've made it because we rent our own apartment now or are no longer sleeping on the couch. Or maybe we have a better car now, but then we plateau and feel like we've reached our peak. It can be difficult to step outside our normal routine to connect with others that we normally don't associate with. Stepping outside of our comfort zone is easier said than done given that most immigrants may have multiple jobs, family, children, and responsibilities to tend to daily. Yet, there is power in association. Just as I explained in the first chapter, who you associate yourself with daily typically can really influence who you become. Therefore, if you are only associating with others that are all starting at zero, struggling to survive, and not aspiring for anything better, then most likely, it will become easier for you to settle and also have low aspirations.

Oranges grow on orange trees and apples grow on apple trees. There are no other fruits that grow on these trees, so remember, to be a hybrid and to be different than the tree you grew from, you must venture out and associate with other trees. Often, this requires creative measures alongside resourcefulness, which is something almost every Hispanic innately has. Over the years, I've learned that the most powerful driving force to extend beyond my comfort zone is to tap into what I do have, look how far I have already come and allow that to fuel my confidence so that I'm not scared to engage into new frontiers. Fear of rejection is one of the biggest obstacles people face when trying to expand their association of people. We all have fears of our own, but the true key to overcoming these fears is to change our focus to what we do have rather than what we don't have.

For example: I may not have attended a four-year university, but I've been all over Latin America installing point to point microwave dishes for over three years. I worked for one of the founding companies who created what we today know as WIFI. I worked at a startup that was one of the pioneers of what we now know as text messaging. I may not have the book education but my field experience in my opinion is much more valuable. I joke and say, "While others were reading books, I was writing them."

It's not difficult to connect with others. All you have to do is find common ground. I call it "humanizing" people. Time and time again throughout my life, I've been able to elevate myself through what may have seemed small opportunities to connect with others simply by first connecting on a human level (Leave the titles out of it) and then once the connection is built, focusing on what I did bring to the table and remaining eager to contribute wherever I could with the experience I did have and my eagerness to learn.

Networking

I often get told I am a "Social Butterfly." This has not always been the case. I've come to realize that one of the keys to my success has been not being afraid to have conversations with people and share my goals and ambitions (Law of attraction) with people. When attending networking events, I look for people gathered in circles, holding their drinks or finger foods in one hand and discussing their professions. In those moments, I take the opportunity to listen and find the right time to share what I aspire to do one day. Say things like, "You know what I've always wanted to do [insert goal/ambition here]." Almost every time I've done this, it has resulted in someone willing to share their experience or even possibly introducing me to someone. In my 25 years in tech, I feel I've only had to "cold" interview for my first job. I have navigated my career from one company to another being referred by previous peer or boss. Creating connections, real relationships that aren't just surface level for yourself will change your life and level of success. There's always somebody that knows somebody that needs someone to get something done. The point is, getting out of hermit mode and socializing with the right people is detrimental. Having a genuine conversation is important when networking. Sometimes, the title of a person can be intimidating, creating a barrier to entry. To overcome this, it's helpful to remove the title and focus on common interests and shared experiences. For example, discussing family, children, and sports can help establish a connection.

In today's world we no longer must rely on the strings of hope that we bump into the right person who can help us. Everything we need to elevate is only a swipe or button away through social media. Unfortunately, many of us aren't utilizing social media to elevate the way we should and that is where creativity and resourcefulness can help you to think outside of the box. There's one strategy that I've used throughout the years that still works for me to this day to connect with people that I otherwise wouldn't be able to. For example, if I attended an event and really enjoyed the keynote speaker and wanted to connect but couldn't because as expected he or she were swarmed by other people after. Rather than storming the stage after the talk I found a different more memorable approach to connect. I'd find them on Linkedin the next day and would request to add them to my network and then would message them thanking them for chatting with me after their talk and asking them if they'd be open to either coffee or a follow up conversation over video or a phone call. The truth is they probably won't remember if they talked to you or not and may even feel a bit guilty for not remembering you. In almost every case I have successfully landed a follow up interaction with the person. These messages tend to rise above the others in the DMs and usually have a high response rate.

Additionally, I'll search for people on Linkedin who share connections with me and will reach out letting them know that we have a lot of similar people in our network, and I'd love to connect and see if there is a way, I could support what they're doing. That's another intro that always opens a door to connect. I've always made it a point to give more than I receive in any relationship, but especially when creating a network for yourself, it is key. You're only as good as the network that you've created, because within your network are the opportunities, you're looking for within the people that you seek. Remember, it's not how many people you know, it's how many people know you. For example, it's not about how many connections follow you on LinkedIn, it's how many of them will answer your phone call when you call or how many of them will respond to your emails.

Being motivated to attend events with speakers and connecting with them is a great way to start networking. As a student, you have the freedom to connect with your professors and guest speakers on LinkedIn. Remember, everyone is connected in some way. It's like the game people played years ago, "Five Degrees from Kevin Bacon," where it's said you are only five connections away from someone who knows Kevin Bacon (US Actor). With LinkedIn, it's even easier, and probably could be accomplished in only taking two or three steps. It's funny because I've become good friends with Jose Hernández, who used to seem unreachable to me. I remember seeing him at conferences and even forcing myself to the front at a presentation he gave at San Jose State so my daughter could take a picture with him. Now, we've become friends, our families know each other and even agreed to author the Foreword for this book. This is all the result of strategic networking.

Elevator Speech

As immigrants, many of us are taught to keep our heads down, work hard, don't boast or brag about our accomplishments, and to remain humble. The problem with this is that if nobody knows what you've done or where you'd like to go then nobody knows how to help. Therefore, there can be people that you've met that could possibly benefit from what you do or may know someone that needs what you do which means an opportunity for you, but you missed it because you didn't speak up when you met them. It's unfortunate that our misinterpretation of what it means to be humble has us not fully showing up correctly in the necessary arenas. With that said, I'd like to challenge you to think about how you describe yourself when you first meet people, regardless of whether you've established a professional career yet or not. This is what is called your elevator pitch. You should never just meet someone and give them your name. You have the first eleven seconds upon meeting someone to make an impactful impression.

Imagine this: you step into an elevator, ready to make a lasting impression on a potential investor, client, or mentor. In that brief moment, you have the opportunity to deliver an elevator pitch that captures their attention and leaves a lasting impact.

With just a few seconds to spare, you must articulate your business, product, or your goals/ambitions in a clear and compelling manner. Your words should paint a vivid picture and convey the essence of your purpose and vision. An elevator pitch is a concise and compelling summary of who you are, what you do, and what value you can bring to others. It is called an elevator pitch because it should be short enough to deliver in the time it takes to ride an elevator, typically around 30 seconds to two minutes. When you are done delivering your elevator pitch, the person you are speaking to should have a question to learn more and feel leaving them inspired to want to be a part of whatever it is that you are doing. The elevator pitch is your golden ticket to success in the fast-paced world of business. But why is the elevator pitch so crucial? It is the difference between being forgotten in the sea of mediocrity and standing out as a beacon of innovation and potential. It is the gateway to opportunity, the key that unlocks doors previously closed. In a world saturated with information overload, the elevator pitch cuts through the noise, commanding attention and leaving a lasting impression. It showcases your ability to articulate your value proposition, your unique selling point, and your passion in a concise and impactful manner.

Here's an example of my elevator speech if I'm trying to land a speaking opportunity:

"Hi, my name is Carlos Quezada, a seasoned Latino exec currently serving as the Vice President of Customer Experience and Digital Engagement for a global Fortune 100 tech giant. I have 25 years of tech industry expertise; I've proudly earned the title of Top 100 Most Influential Latinos in Tech for three consecutive years. My journey, starting in Degollado, Jalisco, Mexico, and arriving in the US at 14, has been anything but conventional. Climbing the corporate ladder to VP has been a testament to resilience. I consider myself blessed and driven by purpose—to uplift fellow Latinos and immigrants. Actively involved in the local Hispanic community, I'm committed to motivating, educating, and fostering success for all and looking to share my knowledge, experience and insights with your audience."

You see, creating an elevator pitch for yourself involves a few key steps. First, you need to identify your unique selling points or strengths that set you apart from others. This could be your skills, experience, or specific accomplishments. Next, you should think about your target audience and what they would find valuable or interesting about you. Tailoring your pitch to their needs and interests will make it more effective.

Once you have these elements, you can start crafting your pitch. Begin with a captivating opening that grabs attention and clearly states who you are and what you do. Then, highlight your unique selling points and explain how they can benefit your audience. Finally, end with a strong call to action, such as inviting them to connect with you or learn more about your work.

Remember, practice is key to delivering a confident and impactful elevator pitch. Rehearse it until it feels natural and authentic and be prepared to adapt it based on different situations or audiences. We set ourselves up for success by being prepared. Oprah Winfrey defined success as being opportunity meeting preparation, and I couldn't have said it better. Preparation is really the extra factor that pushes you beyond your limits into rooms and with the right people who will help take you to the next level. Remember, success is not a destination but a continuous process of growth and development. There's always more to learn and areas that need improvement in our lives. There should never be a time where you are not striving for more or setting the bar even higher. So, take charge of your life, embrace change, and strive for greatness. Elevate yourself, and the possibilities are endless.

REFLECTION QUESTION

Create your elevator pitch right here. Think of not only what you do professionally, but what your current goals are, and what you need to get there.

ROCÍO PÉREZ

Creator | Author | Speaker | Trainer

The MindShift Game

THE MINDSHIFT

Shift Your Mind and Grow Your Bottomline

By: Rocío Pérez

What dream have you held onto that scares the living daylights out of you yet simultaneously inspires you to envision what is possible? As a little girl, my greatest dream was to become a teacher. Although the circumstances around me didn't exactly put me on that path, that dream was my escape. It is the dream I took with me wherever I went, and as a young teenage mom, when the walls felt like they were crashing in on me, it was pursuing that dream that saved me.

This journey taught me the importance of owning the roadmap to my life and becoming my very own navigator. I knew I was the only one who could lead the way. I took charge of my direction, even if I needed to figure out exactly how. My end goal was clear - to attend college and become a teacher. This clarity of purpose guided me through my life's most profound and challenging obstacles.

At 15, I knew I had to take immediate, drastic action to create an opportunity for my son and me to flourish. Despite facing obstacles like being underage and the need to emancipate myself to attend university, I remained steadfast in my vision. I connected with an older mentor who helped me navigate the process of divorcing from my parents to pursue my educational dreams. This experience taught me the importance of leading from the bottom up, clearly communicating my needs and goals to those who could support me on my journey, and understanding that there will be many people to help me along the way and that I was the only one who held the roadmap, a treasure map to my future. This hard-learned lesson taught me perseverance and self-reliance. Success comes from taking ownership of my path and continually evolving into the person I need to be to achieve my goals.

My leadership program will help you gain insights into self-efficacy, learn effective self-regulation strategies, and reflect on a personalized self-care plan. Self-efficacy is the belief that you can bring your desires to fruition. It equips you with the capacity to navigate challenges, reduce stress, and cultivate positive relationships. It leads to a more fulfilling and meaningful life. It empowers you to handle stress, overcome obstacles, and foster connections effectively. By exercising self-efficacy, individuals can strengthen and develop crucial qualities such as self-awareness, empathy, and resilience. These qualities are vital for maintaining a healthy and balanced life. Self-efficacy components, including self-care, self-awareness, self-reflection, self-discovery, and self-regulation, will help you achieve everything you dream of.

Making my dream a reality required me to maintain a growth mindset and understand self-efficacy. By doing this, I constantly sought unorthodox ways to educate myself to evolve into the best version of myself. I acknowledge that I am always in the process of becoming, so I prioritize investing in my learning through seminars, conversations, and experiences that challenge and broaden my perspective. I make it a point to surround myself with more knowledgeable and experienced individuals, as being the least educated person in the room is a sign of growth and learning.

Most importantly, the key to educating ourselves is to approach education as a key to learning more about who we are as individuals. We can lead ourselves only by tapping into the internal wisdom of who we are. This understanding of self is an essential element in leading others. Many people rush into leadership positions before truly understanding themselves. If we knew ourselves from the inside out, we would live our version of a happier, healthier, and wealthier life. Life reveals to us what is important for us to transcend. That's why it's vital to approach mentorship from a place of curiosity and express gratitude for the times someone triggers or upsets us. Every experience reveals what hides inside us and is ready to heal.

Finally, it is crucial to understand that we can't accomplish something great by working alone. We all need each other. This need for connection is why networking is paramount to elevating yourself wherever you are. Networking has been instrumental in guiding me to where I want to be in life. I proactively built a network for myself long before I needed it, fostering relationships with people from various backgrounds and regions for nearly three decades. Instead of seeking favors, I focused on building genuine connections and supporting others. Networking goes beyond seeking help; it's also about assisting others. Networking becomes mutually beneficial when approached with a mindset of giving rather than taking. For example, when seeking a mentor, it is essential to consider what value I can bring to the relationship. Networking requires introspection and self-awareness, as unresolved issues can negatively impact our interactions with others. By understanding how I can contribute and serve others, networking becomes a platform for growth and collaboration.

If you are starting to network or have been networking for a while, there are a few things that I still am intentional about doing that have helped the success of the relationships I've gained through networking. I learned early on that when I first started networking, I must stand firm and engage in meaningful conversations. I looked people in the eyes, wrote notes on their business cards (back when we used them), and now I save their contact information on my phone. Ensuring we have each other's contact information increases the likelihood of maintaining a solid relationship. Additionally, I made a point to introduce people to each other, fostering connections and expanding my network.

While it's important to network within your neighborhood, it is crucial to remember to network outside of your circle. It's great to do business with people you like; however, sticking to those you're familiar with keeps you inside your comfort zone. Stepping out of that comfort zone and connecting with people outside can open new opportunities and perspectives. You can build meaningful relationships beyond surface-level connections by treating others as individuals first and showing genuine interest in who they are and what they have accomplished. The approach of being interested instead of being "interesting" has been one of the most significant discoveries for me in networking.

None of us are bound to where we were born or are currently. Understanding that a *shift* in our *mindset* dictates the direction our path in life takes is when everything starts to change. This shift may happen differently for everyone, yet the rules are the same. We are responsible for creating the life we want. We can only achieve the means to get there through constant self-discovery fueled by the hunger to evolve into better versions of ourselves. I can help you *shift your mind and grow your bottom line* to achieve your desired success.

CHAPTER 4

IMPOSSIBLE IS NOTHING

"Impossible is just a big word thrown around by small men who ind it easier to live in the world they've been given than to explore the power they have to change it. Impossible is not a fact. It's an opinion. Impossible is not a declaration. It's a dare. Impossible is potential. Impossible is temporary. Impossible is nothing."

Mohammed Ali

After my first wife and I divorced, my life was completely disrupted, and I found myself overwhelmed by sadness and confusion. I felt the weight of despair and uncertainty, as my mind was in constant rewind, replaying events as to how I arrived in the place I was in. However, one morning while ironing my clothes in the room I was renting, I caught a glimpse of an Adidas commercial featuring Mohammed Ali with the slogan, "Impossible is Nothing." This message struck a chord within me and ignited a fire in my soul. I immediately printed it and hung the slogan up on my bathroom mirror and at my desk at work. Little did I know that these words would become my guiding light, leading me on a transformative journey of self-discovery and triumph. At the time, everything in my life seemed impossible, yet, I had to identify the "impossible" in my life, the obstacle that seemed insurmountable.

Identify What Your "Impossible" Is

It became clear to me that my health was the foundation upon which I could rebuild my shattered spirit. Determined to reclaim my physical and mental well-being, I made a conscious decision to embark on a path of self-improvement. I took the first step towards my transformation by joining a local gym. Surrounded by like-minded individuals, I found solace in the camaraderie and support of my newfound fitness community. They became my team, my allies in this uphill battle against my own limitations. With unwavering determination, I committed myself to a rigorous workout routine, pushing my body to its limits and beyond. Each day, I would sweat and strain, feeling the burn in my muscles as I gradually regained my strength and vitality. The gym became my sanctuary, a place where I could channel my frustrations and insecurities into tangible progress.

With the support of my friends from the gym, we tackled the steep grueling hike up Mission Peak in the Bay Area. A hike I had never done or heard of before. This is one of the most intense hikes in the area. The coaches pushed and motivated all of us by applying their 15-step method. The concept was simple yet profound: take 15 steps, and then allow yourself a moment to rest and recharge. Rinse and repeat. Applying this method, I was able to accomplish something I never thought possible-hiking up Mission Peak. After almost two hours I made it to the top. After that, I continued to hike Mission Peak once a month eventually achieving a personal best time of 53 minutes.

15-Step Method

Intrigued by this approach, I decided to apply it to my own life. I realized that just as conquering Mission Peak, required breaking it down into manageable steps, so too did any obstacle in life. Similar to needing the motivation of my gym buddies, I recognized how every person needs this type of encouragement around our goals. We need people around us that encourage and motivate us toward the direction we're headed in. I began to view every challenge as a series of bite-sized pieces, each one leading me closer to my ultimate goal.

The 15-step method became my universal answer in the face of any challenge and adversity. It taught me the importance of breaking everything down into manageable pieces as well as pacing myself and acknowledging that progress is not always linear. Some steps were arduous, testing my resolve and pushing me to my limits. I overcame despair by refusing to succumb to it. One step in a direction away from despair, no matter how painful it is, is one step closer to victory.

Tackling challenges armed with the wisdom of Mohammed Ali and the 15-step method, I conquered not only the physical challenge of hiking Mission Peak but also the emotional and psychological hurdles that accompanied my divorce. I emerged from the darkness, a stronger and more resilient version of myself. I've learned that it truly is a one-size fits all approach to obstacles we call problems.

Since then, I have applied this approach to every obstacle that has crossed my path. Whether it be a daunting work project, a personal setback, or a seemingly impossible dream, I break it down into manageable steps. I remind myself that nothing is truly insurmountable if I approach it with determination, perseverance, and a willingness to take it one step at a time. Through the power of breaking down the "impossible" into bite-sized pieces, I have discovered that the greatest victories are often born from the smallest triumphs. Life's challenges may be daunting, but with the right mindset and a steadfast commitment to progress, I have come to believe that the impossible truly is nothing. Not only is impossible nothing, it's also important to remember, "Do not be a victim of your circumstance." Do not feel sorry for yourself and don't make excuses.

The 15-step method for problem-solving is a structured approach that involves several stages, including defining the problem, gathering information, generating possible solutions, evaluating those solutions, and implementing the best one. Here's a summarized version:

1. Define the problem: Clearly articulate what the issue is.

2. Gather information: Collect relevant data and facts.

3. Analyze the problem: Break down the issue and understand its root causes.

4. Identify potential solutions: Brainstorm possible ways to address the problem.

5. Evaluate solutions: Assess the pros and cons of each solution.

6. Select the best solution: Choose the most feasible and effective option.

7. Plan implementation: Develop a detailed plan for executing the chosen solution.

8. Implement the plan: Put the plan into action.

9. Monitor progress: Keep track of how the solution is being implemented.

10. Gather feedback: Solicit input from stakeholders on the effectiveness of the solution.

11. Make adjustments: Modify the plan as needed based on feedback and changing circumstances.

12. Evaluate outcomes: Assess the results of the implemented solution.

13. Document lessons learned: Record insights gained from the problem-solving process.

14. Share results: Communicate findings and outcomes with relevant parties.

15. Celebrate success: Recognize and acknowledge achievements made in solving the problem.

This method provides a systematic framework for addressing a wide range of problems, from personal challenges to complex organizational issues.

REFLECTION QUESTION

What is a goal that you may feel is impossible to achieve? What are 15 steps you can break it down into to make it more manageable?

CHAPTER 5

BE BOLD

"I like to ask for forgiveness, not permission."

Carlos Quezada

It was my first tech job after graduating from the trade school I attended (M.I.T). I worked as a contractor on the swing shift and was one of the lowest-ranking employees. My main responsibility as a "Network Monitor" was to sit in front of the screens and promptly notify the on-call engineer whenever there was a red alert. It required no thinking, just picking up the phone and making a call. Coincidently, I was also the only person who could speak Spanish in the entire company. Lastly, it's important to note that I also had (and still have) a playful and goofy personality. With all that in mind... One day, while sitting in the NOC (Network Operations Center), I overheard the CEO and vice president of engineering discussing their concerns about a potential partnership in Mexico. They were unsure about how to proceed and handle the logistics. In a lighthearted manner, I jokingly suggested that if they needed a translator, I would be in Mexico for my sister's quinceañera and could help them out. To my surprise, they actually liked the idea. I quickly clarified that I was just kidding and didn't have the experience for such a business meeting. However, they insisted that I join them.

So, I attended my sister's quinceañera in Jalisco, Mexico, and then took a bus to Mexico City. The night before the meeting, we stayed at a luxurious hotel, which was a new experience for me. During dinner, they discussed the strategy for the next day, and it suddenly dawned on me that I hadn't even arranged for my own accommodations. I was only 18, I had never done this before. When I asked where they were staying, they informed me that we were all staying at the same hotel. When they found out I had nowhere to stay, they playfully teased me for not thinking ahead, but they arranged a room for me.

The next day, during the meeting, something unexpected happened. Instead of directing questions to my colleagues, the representatives from the telco company directed their questions to me. I unintentionally took charge of the meeting and ended up driving the entire conversation. After approximately 90 minutes or so, to my amazement, I managed to walk out of the meeting with a provisional nationwide contract. The meeting was with a company named Telcel, the largest cellular provider in all of Mexico. Remember, I was 18. I had never been in a business meeting before. I was wearing the suit I had planned to wear to my sister's quinceañera because I didn't own a business suit. During the meeting, I forgot to translate. I was so excited that I knew the answer to all their questions that I just continued speaking. Rather than being upset, my CEO and VP of engineering encouraged me to continue leading the discussion as they could tell it was going well.

Telcel was thrilled with the meeting outcome. They offered us a provisional agreement stating if I could prove the results, as I had promised them during the meeting within the next six months, they would expand the regional contract to a nationwide contract. This was a significant opportunity because, at that time, we were pioneering what today we call text messaging. No one has been able to send data over the wireless network before and I was about to bring this tech to Mexico as an 18-year-old.

Considering my initial position as the lowest-ranking employee, it was surprising to be entrusted with managing the rollout of this test. I came back from Mexico and was promoted to a permanent employee and promoted to lead the project with Telcel. I spent the next six conducting extensive testing to ensure that our system wouldn't congest their network during peak times. I had previously worked on a similar project, so I knew what needed to be done. Although I was initially just assisting in projects before, my ability to speak Spanish and my willingness to speak up led to my involvement.

At the age of 18, I never imagined that this experience would have such a profound impact on my career. Even now, as I reflect on it, I have children of similar age, and I can't fathom them being in a similar position and being trusted like that. It truly was a remarkable journey. I spent two years in that role, and within that initial six-month window, I successfully completed the initial rollout and spent the next two years bringing text messaging to Mexico.

I wasn't thinking about the pressure or the importance of the situation. My focus was on my curiosity and my belief in my abilities. I didn't realize the gravity of the opportunity at the time, I was just naive and didn't overthink things. I've always had the mindset of taking on new challenges and figuring things out as I go. This experience was just another example of that attitude.

Speak Up for Yourself

Years ago, I worked for a company that was acquired by a much larger, more established company. While working at this company, it always felt like the parent company was making all the important decisions and we had to just go along with them. This bothered many of us because in some cases our company had more innovative ideas, yet we were not being heard or taken into consideration. It seemed counterproductive to adopt the mindset of the larger company.

I realized I couldn't just accept this situation. I had to find a way to show the rest of the company, including the "mothership," that we were ahead of the curve. To do this, I had begun to showcase the work my team was doing and build strong partnerships across the company.

This eventually led to an opportunity for me to present our work in front of the CEO. Well not intentionally. I technically wasn't invited. It was a risky move that could have cost me my job. I had discovered there was a chance that someone else would be taking credit for the work my team and I had worked so hard on in the last five years. I knew I couldn't let that happen. I needed to speak up not only for myself but for my team. I made the bold decision to jump on a plan and attend a workshop where the CEO would be at alongside other top members of the company. I wasn't invited nor did the CEO or my VP know that I would be in attendance. I strategically connected with some of the leaders I was familiar with. I also confided them the reason for me showing up to the meeting. They were very supportive and were instrumental in me getting a spot on the calendar the next day as a guest speaker. It was my time to speak up for my team and was able to showcase what we had done and provide ideas on how to make everything more efficient.

After my presentation, I was praised for the work the team had done. The presentation went well, and I succeeded in elevating my team in front of the most senior leaders of the company. The meeting went so well that I left the meeting with getting permanently invited to these meetings going forward and was two huge initiatives that gave my team a space to be heard and have an extensive impact. This experience taught me the importance of building strong partnerships, taking bold actions, and coupling it with using my voice. Once again, it was validated to me that passively sitting by and allowing others to make the rules and set the limits for you only happens when you are not brave enough to be bold and speak up. Change can be made in whatever situation you may find yourself, in what you are not happy with, but more than likely it will require you to speak up. It showed me that by doing so, I can overcome any obstacle and make a significant impact in my career and the lives of others. It was this bold move that also elevated my visibility within the leadership team. This action eventually landed me a promotion to Vice President. Not only did I get elevated but my promotion also helped elevate the rest of my team.

Finding Your Rabbit

I always advise people to view their current actions as an interview for future opportunities. It's important to have a clear vision of where you want to be in your career and to identify individuals who are already in that position as your inspiration. These individuals can serve as your "rabbit," just like in dog racing where a rabbit is a lure that other dogs chase. By tracking their progress and learning from them, you can eventually surpass them and achieve your goals.

To find your rabbit, you need to determine the role you want to have in the next few years and then figure out the steps you need to take to bridge the gap between where you are now and where you want to be. This involves setting specific goals and creating a plan to achieve them. By constantly evaluating your progress and making adjustments along the way, you can ensure that you are moving closer to your desired career outcome.

So, ask yourself: What is your rabbit? What do you envision happening in your career over the years? And will this opportunity bring you closer to that goal? By keeping these questions in mind and actively working towards your aspirations, you can make meaningful progress in your career and achieve the success you desire.

REFLECTION QUESTION

What do you envision happening in your career over the years?

CATALINA PEÑA
Founder and Lead Career Coach

DARING TO DREAM

By: Catalina Peña

When you have children, nurturing their dreams is one of the most important things you can do. Reflecting on my own mother, I saw first-hand the impact of having your past dreams become your lived reality. Despite her strength and love, she had to set aside her aspirations, leaving her dreams shattered. Witnessing her fear of dreaming again, I realized the influence it had on me, shaping my perspective on life as a constant cycle of work and anxiety. It wasn't until I surrounded myself with people who embrace dreaming as an everlasting way of life that I began to question my own desires and aspirations. As mothers, especially from immigrant backgrounds, we hold the responsibility of fostering a sense of wonder and possibility in our children, breaking free from survivalist mentalities to embrace entrepreneurship and limitless potential.

Being a first-generation immigrant myself, I arrived in the United States at the age of nine, facing a unique set of challenges. Due to my family circumstances, I found myself in a constant race against time, where I had to advocate for myself and put myself out there, even when it felt uncomfortable or scary. With no clear roadmap and a turbulent household, I took on the responsibility of ensuring my academic success without much guidance. Originally from Colombia, I navigated through life with a sense of independence, constantly seeking out help from strangers who seemed to be in a better position to offer support. This approach became second nature to me, as I understood that my family couldn't provide the guidance I needed to succeed in the new ways I was envisioning. It wasn't until I began working with professionals that I realized the rarity of my proactive mindset.

In Latin and immigrant households, there is often a cultural emphasis on staying within our own community and not reaching out to strangers for help. This mindset can hinder our progress, as we can only go as far as our community has gone, and we can't grow within our comfort zone. Dreams recognized require people bigger than us, so it is essential to break out of this mentality and seek connections outside of our immediate circle, as these individuals may hold the key to our success in areas such as tech, generational wealth, networking, and most importantly, reaching our dreams.

Many people are taught to work hard and wait for recognition, but the reality is that corporate America can be political and akin to high school cliques. It is crucial to actively network, showcase your talents, and connect with individuals who can help you reach your goals, regardless of how uncomfortable or addy scary it may feel at first.

Many times, in the Latin community we're taught that networking is fake, however, that perception couldn't be further from the truth.

Successful people understand that nothing great is ever accomplished alone. Networking is not about being fake, but rather about building authentic relationships with those who understand this and who inspire and challenge you.

Mentorship is another crucial component to success, and again is often misunderstood as a one-sided power dynamic, but in reality, it can be a mutually beneficial relationship. By approaching mentorship from a relational standpoint rather than a transactional one, you can find mentors who are genuinely invested in your growth and development, and who also need your help in whatever area of expertise you may have. It is important to seek mentors who align with your values and goals, as this will lead to more meaningful and impactful guidance.

A wonderful example of this, is the relationship between me and the author of this book, Carlos, a vice president of a multibillion-dollar company. There was a surprising nervousness on both sides because he was a big executive at a huge company, something I've never done, and I was an entrepreneur, something he never had accomplished. Despite our differing positions, we both found value in each other's perspectives. I was at a stage in my professional journey where I lacked experience in coaching executives, which made me feel insecure. So, I decided to offer my coaching services for free to support in him a pivotal moment of growth and to gain valuable experience and knowledge. It was a mutually beneficial exchange that allowed both of us to learn and grow. This experience helped me understand even more that mentorship should be viewed through the lens of connection rather than power dynamics. It took time for me to recognize the unique value I could offer, especially in a coaching capacity. Many individuals underestimate their own worth and potential impact on others. By approaching someone with admiration and authenticity, regardless of titles or positions, you can truly make a difference in their day and inspire them to go above and beyond for you. The key to effective mentorship lies in the deep authenticity and intentionality behind the connection, fostering a relationship that goes beyond just a formal mentorship arrangement.

When I started the entrepreneurial journey as a coach, it was definitely scary and uncomfortable because it was a new world for me. As I pondered my financial situation, uncertainty clouded my mind. I questioned, how would I manage to pay my rent? How could I navigate through the challenges ahead? Despite the doubts and fears, I knew I couldn't settle for a life of scarcity. I had to seek out abundance, even when it seemed out of reach. It was essential to cultivate a mindset of prosperity, regardless of my current financial status. I understood the rarity of finding peace in such circumstances. Yet, I believed it was crucial for my well-being. Reflecting on my mother's financial wisdom, even through times of homelessness and financial hardship. I felt grateful for the example of grit she set. However, venturing into entrepreneurship presented new challenges that tested my resolve. Despite moments of doubt and shame, I learned to trust in the universe's provision. Embracing the unknown and believing in my own safety became a daily practice. It was a constant battle against the instinctual urge to revert to survival mode and desperation. However, I am aware that without constantly reassuring myself of my safety and well-being, I risk not truly believing in it. And without that belief, my body may resist the abundance and success that come my way, questioning its authenticity and my worthiness of it. Making our dreams a reality is very possible, no matter where you're at, or what situation you're born into, but first you must truly believe. It's that mindset shift that will bring it into fruition.

CHAPTER 6

IMPOSTER SYNDROME

"When you know you're ENOUGH!

When you stop focusing on
all things that you're not.

When you stop fussing over perceived flaws.

When you remove all imposed and unbelievable
expectations on yourself.

When you start celebrating yourself more.

When you focus on all that you are.

When you start believing that your perceived
flaws are just that - perception."

—Malebo Sephodi

We all know that imposter syndrome is a tough and debilitating feeling that can affect anyone. But it seems to be particularly prevalent among those who have come from poverty and difficult childhoods, especially first-generation immigrants, like me, who have come to America in search of a better life. We are, driven by a burning desire to elevate ourselves and our families, and often find ourselves struggling to fit in or belong among the very people we aspire to be around.

Even though I've coached and mentored others in my teams, workplaces, and community to navigate their goals despite imposter syndrome, I have also battled with it myself and continue to do so.

Overcoming imposter syndrome has been a journey of self-discovery and embracing the unique path that brought me to where I am today. Despite being named one of the Top 100 Most Influential Latinos in Tech, I've grappled with many moments of self-doubt. My career trajectory, born from a humble origin in Mexico, and navigating a move to the U.S. at 14, has been far from conventional.

Climbing the corporate ladder to reach the position of Vice President at a global high-tech company was a testament to perseverance and resilience. Yet, imposter syndrome has a way of creeping in, questioning whether I truly belong at this level of success. However, I've learned to combat these doubts by reflecting on my journey, acknowledging the diversity of experiences that shape my unique perspective. The diversity of thought that I bring to all decisions based on my experience is invaluable.

So why is imposter syndrome so common among those who have overcome tremendous odds? Well, it all comes down to the stark contrast between where we came from and where we want to be. The difference between our humble beginnings and the environments we now find ourselves in can be overwhelming, leading to a constant fear of being exposed as a fraud. We question whether we truly deserve our achievements and whether we truly belong in the circles we now navigate.

But here's the thing - there is hope. While imposter syndrome may never completely go away, we can learn to manage it through deliberate action and self-improvement. The key is to recognize that confidence is not something we're born with, but rather a skill that can be developed through hard work, dedication, and faith.

By investing time and effort into honing our skills and continuously working on ourselves, we can gradually gain the confidence we need to thrive. The more we immerse ourselves in our chosen field, the more expertise we gain, and the more secure we feel in our abilities. This newfound confidence acts as a shield against the self-doubt that plagues us, allowing us to show up fully and seize the opportunities that come our way.

Of course, overcoming imposter syndrome is not without its challenges. Our minds can be treacherous, filled with self-sabotaging thoughts and limiting beliefs. It's all too easy to get lost in a maze of negative self-talk, talking ourselves out of opportunities and succumbing to the paralyzing grip of imposter syndrome.

To navigate imposter syndrome, it's crucial to develop strategies that counteract the negative self-talk and foster a positive mindset. Surrounding ourselves with a supportive network of mentors, peers, and allies who understand the unique challenges we face can provide a lifeline in times of doubt. Sharing experiences and seeking guidance from those who have walked a similar path can offer reassurance, validation and perspective, reminding us that we're not alone in our struggles.

One thing that has always been important to me is being transparent and open about my thoughts and goals regardless of how much they may scare me because the bigger the dream, the more fear we should feel. As a result, I'm not afraid to speak up and take on tasks that others might shy away from. I'm willing to do the grunt work and get my hands dirty. I've noticed that many of my immigrant mentees share a similar perspective. We often find ourselves being recognized for going above and beyond in our jobs, even though we feel like we're just doing what we're supposed to do. This shows that our minimum expectation, most of the time, surpasses other's maximum because we feel the need to prove ourselves. So, for me, it's about embracing that mindset and not being afraid to put in the extra effort and allow that hard work to keep me moving to defeat any insecurity or negative self-talk that I may have.

Additionally, cultivating a growth mindset and embracing the concept of lifelong learning can be instrumental in combating imposter syndrome. Recognizing that success is not a destination, but a continuous journey allows us to view setbacks and failures as opportunities for growth rather than evidence of our inadequacy. By reframing challenges as steppingstones to success, we can build resilience and develop a sense of self-assurance that withstands the onslaught of imposter syndrome.

Even if you've never heard the name for it but can resonate with what I'm describing, just know that you're not alone. The imposter syndrome monster is real, but you can take away its power. Here are my thoughts on how to help keep the imposter syndrome monster in the closet:

Embrace Your Journey: Recognize that your path, is inherently unique. Embrace the diverse experiences, challenges, and triumphs that have shaped your professional story. Remember, success is often a result of navigating unconventional routes, and your journey adds depth and value to any situation or decision that needs to be made.

Celebrate Achievements: Take the time to celebrate your successes, both big and small. Acknowledge your achievements, and don't downplay your contributions. Each milestone is a testament to your skills, dedication, and the positive impact you bring to the tech industry.

Cultivate a Supportive Network: Surround yourself with mentors, peers, and allies who understand the unique challenges faced by immigrants in the tech world. Share your experiences, seek guidance, and build a supportive community that reinforces your worth. Having a network that understands and appreciates your journey can provide invaluable encouragement during moments of self-doubt.

Continuous Learning and Growth: Imposter syndrome often thrives in the fear of being exposed as a fraud. Combat this by investing in your professional development. Stay curious, seek opportunities for learning, and embrace challenges as opportunities for growth. The more you invest in expanding your skills, the more confident you'll become in your abilities, eroding the imposter syndrome's foundation.

Give Back and Mentor: Pay forward the support you've received by helping other immigrants in the tech industry. Actively participate in mentorship programs, share your experiences, and provide guidance to those who may be navigating similar challenges. By contributing to the success of others, you reinforce your own value and break the cycle of imposter syndrome, realizing that you are not only deserving of your achievements but also capable of inspiring others to reach their full potential.

REFLECTION QUESTION

What specific achievements, skills, or qualities do you possess that others might value or see as significant contributions? How can you remind yourself of these strengths in moments of self-doubt?

OSCAR GARCIA
Chief Empowerment Officer
at Aspira Consulting

5 DAILY LIFE FACTORS THAT CAN CONTRIBUTE TO IMPOSTER SYNDROME IN THE U.S.

By Oscar Garcia

Are you feeling like a misfit, constantly doubting your abilities, and fearing that someone will find out you are not as smart or capable as they think. If so, you may be struggling with imposter syndrome. This condition is surprisingly common, affecting many professionals. But what causes it, and how can we overcome its effects? To help you, I'll go over key factors that contributed to my feeling of imposter syndrome at UC Berkeley and how they made me feel inferior or not smart enough. Stay tuned while I talk about this hurdle we often come across!

Imposter Syndrome in a Word

Inadequate. Imposter syndrome - you must have heard this term a lot lately, but what does it mean? Simply put, imposter syndrome is the feeling of being an inadequate or an unworthy person, despite evidence to the contrary. This can manifest in many ways, such as feeling like you're not qualified for your job or that you're only successful because the company gave you special treatment.

For some people, imposter syndrome is a chronic condition that affects their everyday lives. Others may only experience it in certain situations, such as when starting a new job or giving a presentation. I went through my bout of feeling imposter syndrome freshman year at UC Berkeley. I was placed in remedial English class because, supposedly my writing and reading skills were deficient. Yet, I received As in English all four years of high school. I internalized the feeling that I was not smart enough, and that I didn't belong at Cal.

While imposter syndrome can be painful, frustrating, and demoralizing, it's important to remember that many highly successful people experience imposter syndrome at some point in their life.

Top Factors that Trigger Imposter Syndrome

Do you find yourself feeling insufficient, despite your qualifications and accomplishments? If so, you might be going through imposter syndrome. But what are the factors that contribute to imposter syndrome in us? When I started putting more thought into my self-doubt during my college days, I found these top 5 things to be my biggest triggers:

1. Comparisons in All Forms

It's all too easy to fall into the trap of constantly comparing ourselves to others. We see what they have and what they've achieved, and it can make us feel like we're not good enough. We start to doubt our abilities and accomplishments, wondering if we're cut out for this. The key at this point is to remember that everyone has unique talents and strengths. Comparison is only going to hold you back. Once I pinpointed that my habit of comparing myself to other college students was making me doubt my capabilities, a switch flipped in me. That's when I decided to focus on my journey and trust that I have what it takes to achieve my goals.

2. The Pressure of Perfectionism

Many of us strive for perfection in everything we do, which can harm our mental health. When we're constantly trying to make everything perfect, we're setting ourselves up for disappointment and feelings of inadequacy. This can lead to imposter syndrome, where we feel like we're not good enough or a fake. We may start to second-guess our abilities and hesitate to take risks. If you're struggling with perfectionism, it's important to remember that nobody is perfect. We all make mistakes, and that's okay. Accepting our imperfections is an essential step in managing imposter syndrome. Try to focus on your successes rather than your failures and give yourself credit for your hard work and efforts. Remember that activity beats perfection.

3. Fear of Failure

Another big reason we might feel insufficient is the constant pressure to succeed. We're constantly being told that we must do our best and be the best. As a first-generation professional, we shoulder the responsibility for our family's sacrifices and success. Unfortunately, this pressure can lead to a fear of failure. When we're afraid of failing, it's easy to believe we're not good enough. After all, if we were smart or talented, we wouldn't be afraid of failing, right? Wrong. Imposter syndrome doesn't mean that you're not good enough - it just means that you're human and capable of feeling scared and uncertain sometimes.

4. Lack of Self-Confidence

A big part of imposter syndrome is a lack of self-confidence. We doubt our skills and wonder if we can do the things we have accomplished. This can lead us to feel like we are always one step away from being found out as incapable and not-so-smart. If we can work on building our self-confidence, it can help us to overcome imposter syndrome and believe in ourselves more. Talking to a therapist or counselor can help in this area because they'll provide guidance and support as you build your self-confidence.

5. Internalized Shame and Bias

Internalized shame and fear can lead us to believe that we're somehow undeserving of our accomplishments. Moreover, societal bias contributes to imposter syndrome by telling us that we must be perfect to succeed. I also believe imposter syndrome is often perpetuated by a lack of mentorship and support.

We worry that we will be exposed as frauds or odd ones and that our actual lack of talent or ability will be revealed. This can result in anxiety, depression, and a feeling of powerlessness. But it doesn't have to be this way because we can choose to believe in ourselves and our abilities.

Conclusion

It's normal to feel like an imposter at some point in our life. After all, we're constantly bombarded with images and messages telling us we're not good enough. Whether in school, work, or in our personal life, we're constantly comparing ourselves to others. I want you to know that with all your talents and imperfections, you are good enough. You have the qualities to succeed. If you're still doubting yourself, start by identifying your trigger points and then devise a strategy to overcome them.

CHAPTER 7

AUTHENTIC LEADERSHIP

"It's only lonely at the top if you don't bring anyone with you."

Carlos Quezada

Authentic leadership transcends mere management; it embodies a genuine and transparent connection between leaders and their teams. Authentic leaders are true to themselves, guided by a strong sense of integrity, and unafraid to reveal their values, vulnerabilities, and personal stories.

This open and honest approach has always helped me foster trust, creating a workplace culture where individuals feel valued and understood. I always try to prioritize the well-being of my teams, recognizing and appreciating the unique strengths each member brings. I try to actively listen, and engage in meaningful communication, inspiring a shared commitment to a common goal or vision. Essentially, to me, authentic leadership is about being true to one's values, embracing authenticity as a strength, and cultivating an environment where individuals can flourish and contribute their best work.

Throughout my career, I have made it a priority to establish a strong sense of vulnerability and openness with my teams. I believe in fostering an environment where team members feel comfortable and view me as an equal rather than just a boss. This approach has consistently resulted in the formation of close-knit, family-like teams.

Initially, some individuals struggle with implementing these practices. To address this, I humanize the leadership experience by removing formality and injecting fun into the workplace. I'm probably one of the most unconventional executives, because I prioritize enjoyment at work, and I attribute that to being one of the reasons my team at our company has had so much success. We're having fun with everything we do, and we don't take ourselves too seriously. However, as the leader, I must set that tone and help enable that environment by leading with vulnerability, authenticity, and support. These are three traits that many immigrants share

Vulnerability

One of my coworkers shared a story with me recently. He said, "I remember when I joined this company and relocated from Guadalajara to Palo Alto. I was in a room with all the senior leaders, wearing my blazer and feeling like I finally knew how to work with executives. But then you came along, and everything changed. Previously, we weren't supposed to write an email to a VP without having a few people review it. But watching you casually approach everyone has completely shifted my perception of working with executives." Him telling me that really paraphrased what leadership is all about- authenticity through vulnerability.

Humanizing ourselves by showing up as ourselves and not our title. This is how we build trust and connections with those around us who are looking to us to lead. One example of how I do this is, during team meetings, I dedicate the first few minutes to casual conversations about weekends, family, and even playful banter. This normalization of the environment ensures that team members feel at ease and confident in sharing their thoughts without fear of chastisement or reprimand for mistakes.

When it comes to building relationships and being authentic, my philosophy is all about treating everyone with respect and equality, regardless of where they stand in the company. I've got friends at all levels, from the kitchen staff to the CEO, and I make it a point to talk to everyone in the same way. This approach has really paid off for me and my team, as we've gained a lot of respect and recognition throughout the company.

Now, as for how I learned to be this way, I've had quite a diverse range of jobs throughout my career. I didn't just jump into this role right after college. I've worked my way up and have experienced pretty much every job in between. This has given me a deep understanding of the different roles and responsibilities within the company. I firmly believe in leading by example and never asking my team to do something that I wouldn't do myself. Drawing on my past experiences, I've been able to create a management team that's effective, values each other, and provides support when needed.

Authenticity

Authenticity stands as the cornerstone of effective leadership, fostering trust and connection within your team. Being authentic transcends titles and positions, creating an environment where honesty and transparency thrive. When people authentically share their values, experiences, and even vulnerabilities, it establishes a relatable and genuine connection with their team. This openness cultivates a culture where team members feel safe to express their ideas, voice concerns, and contribute wholeheartedly.

Moreover, authenticity is the foundation of integrity. People who stay true to their principles, even in the face of challenges, build a foundation of trust with their teams. This trust is a catalyst for collaboration and innovation, as team members are more likely to take risks and share innovative ideas when they believe their leader is genuinely invested in their success.

SUPPORT

Another crucial aspect of authentic leadership is providing unconditional support to the team. I empower my team members to make decisions with confidence. I emphasize that as long as they are making decisions aligned with the goal or vision and they are respectful and genuine, I will always stand behind their decisions wholeheartedly. This approach builds trust and encourages team members to represent both me and the team in various settings.

I always tell my team that it's not about the circumstances or the outcomes. So, if they make a decision in a meeting without me and someone criticizes their decision without even knowing what it was, I will support them 100%. As long as they are not being rude or disrespectful, I will stand behind them and their decision, even if it turns out to be wrong. I want them to feel empowered to represent me and the team in any situation and to build trust. I believe in being authentic and acknowledging my own weaknesses. I see myself more as a coach than just someone driving revenue and pushing initiatives. My commitment is to the team, not just the company. I want everyone on my team to have the opportunity to grow and advance in their careers. Now, if I were to talk to my 19-year-old self about authentic leadership, I would emphasize the importance of starting with oneself. It's easy to feel like you must fake it until you make it, but that approach can take away from your authenticity as a leader. Instead, it's about being willing to engage and not being afraid to show who you truly are.

Lastly, it's important to recognize that a leader is not determined by your title. Anyone can be a leader. Remember, a leader inspires and motivates a team while promoting a shared sense of purpose. In contrast, a people manager focuses on organizing tasks, assigning responsibilities, and ensuring efficiency, often emphasizing processes and structures to achieve specific outcomes.

REFLECTION QUESTION

How can I ensure that my actions and decisions align with my values and beliefs, so that I can inspire and empower others?

JESSE CORTEZ

Chief Diversity Officer for a Fortune 10 company

LEADING WITH A LASTING IMPACT: Building A Legacy Through Leadership

By: Jesse Cortez

Imagine that you were given the incredible power to determine your fate, would you take it? Or what if you were gifted a magic pen that could write your legacy and create benefit for others, your family and those closest to you – would you explore it? As this opportunity presented itself, how would you go about making your choices and what would you be willing to sacrifice to get it? Choice *and* sacrifice. Even without superpowers or magic pens, these two words are eternally and closely connected to everything we do. Every choice made, big or small, intentional or unintentional, blazes a path forward. And it's in these decisions that will shape your impact and, ultimately, lead to building a legacy. So, yes, impact *and* legacy are just as intertwined as well.

We know legacy, impact, and leadership can seem like daunting and elusive concepts. However, it is difficult to define success without them. So, how do we bring all of this to life for someone who may be starting a new career or who may be going through a transition without feeling like it is too big of a hill to climb? Like all challenges, we must break it down to its most manageable part(s) to establish a foundation. Primary in this process is finding a source of long-term inspiration that could serve as the anchor to your day-to-day decisions. When applied consistently over time, it will be your guiding star and the 'why' in your motivation on this journey. Chances are that your source of inspiration is likely already at your fingertips as well.

As for me – the oldest of four siblings – I have always felt a strong sense of responsibility to pave the way for my family and ensure a brighter future for them. And it is this connection that prompted me to contemplate the concept of legacy. While many view legacy as how people remember you long after you are gone, I see it differently. To me, legacy is about understanding your history and recognizing the sacrifices others have made to bring you to where you are today. This nuanced view anchors me and it is the source of my motivation in contributing lasting impact on future generations. In other words, I don't want my ancestors' efforts to go to waste on my account. This is the basis of my story, and you have one as well; we all do. Embracing your origins is in large part your opportunity to better understand what shapes the values that can propel you towards a desired destination or goal.

So, what about my story? Well, it is grounded in a tale of two grandfathers. My paternal grandfather was a rather humble and quiet man. A product of simple meals and long, hard days, he was described as a strong, yet thin-framed individual. Shortly after starting his family, he made the incredibly difficult decision to leave Mexico, alone, in search of employment in the United States. His decision to leave his young family in hopes of reuniting must have weighed on him tremendously, especially against the difficult backdrop of the Great Depression and the timing of the Second World War.

As my dad recalled, it was the lowest of the lows for my grandfather when he was down to a mere ten cents and still had no job prospects. Hope and perseverance must have battled the fear and doubt that rested on his shoulders in search of a better life and the desire to reunite his family. So, one night in the streets of San Antonio, Texas, he spent a nickel on three bananas – it was dinner that night. He spent the other five cents on a ticket to the picture show at a theater. However, this ticket wasn't intended for watching the movie; it served as his shelter that night. Despite the uncertainties that must have plagued him, the tide turned in his favor when he secured a job as a ranch hand. This opportunity provided him with a small home where he could reside with his family. Shortly after, his wife (my grandmother), baby girl (my aunt), and 2-year-old son (my father) were reunited.

In a similar vein, my maternal grandfather sought opportunity in the United States as well. While the motivation was similar, his path was a very different one. His mindset, entrepreneurial spirit, and sense of adventure set him apart from others. He was comfortable with risk and his stories were always full of optimism. As a teenaged small-town merchant in Mexico, he learned the value of hard work and integrity. By the time he married and started his family of eight, he ultimately made the decision to immigrate and build inroads into the United States as a migrant worker. Reflecting on his stories, I pictured him moving with the 'picking seasons' throughout different states around the country, whether in California, Minnesota or Florida. While some see risk and uncertainty in his decision, he saw it as an opportunity and a quest to build something more for his family through his sacrifice. Their stories and decisions serve as my source of inspiration and the lifetime of sacrifices they made along the way give me a sense of duty to ensure our collective efforts will continue to create impact *through* me. This is my motivation, my 'why', my origin story.

Today, as a senior leader in a Fortune 10 company, I learned along the way to consistently connect day-to-day interactions to my 'why'. As a result, decision making got easier, which led to higher performance and greater personal fulfillment. The most critical elements for me have been self-awareness, reframing failure as learnings and integrating work and life together. Self-awareness is not always a natural ability for everyone, but it is a skill that can be mastered. When those moments surface and you feel out of place, or you are conscious of how others may perceive you – that feeling is your clue to engage with your audience, co-workers or environment differently. Use your 'why' to give you purpose and confidence in those interactions to be your authentic self. By accepting and valuing ourselves, we – in turn – embrace other's differences too. Positive impact on others surfaces as a result. It also serves as an example for those who may be following in your footsteps to do the same, thereby building meaningful relationships that matter.

For me, seeking to be a role model for my younger cousins by attending higher education sometimes left me feeling lonely and 'on my own'. As one of the first to graduate from college on my mom's side of the family, almost all of my cousins followed in those footsteps. While setting this example for my cousins to follow, it also led to other strings of firsts for me, like first to a master's degree, first to a corporate job, and first to an executive role. Without the 'why' at my core, making a meaningful impact on others through these experiences would have been lost. Acknowledge this aspect and let it fuel you.

Another valuable lesson for me came in reframing failure as a 'learning' instead. These learnings would help me deliver better with each future opportunity. This concept is the second of these critical principles. As a perfectionist, I struggled with anything that was even perceived as a failure. We all face different challenges. My team, my children, and those I mentor are no different. So, I preach to them the importance of using this new knowledge (what we learn when things don't go exactly our way) as building blocks towards progress. The most significant growth occurs when times are challenging, and you are confronted with adversity. It is during these difficult times that you must find a way to overcome obstacles, and these experiences provide valuable lessons. Thus, I never refer to these experiences as failures; instead, I view them as opportunities to learn.

Throughout my career, there have been pivotal moments where I recall a situation or a conversation that highlighted this reality. Most of these came during difficult scenarios where no simple answers or solutions existed. Through these learnings, I was better prepared for the next challenge and people took notice. With goals of reaching vice president at a Fortune 50 company by the age of 40, that dream slipped away from me. However, through these lessons and experience, I emerged stronger and ultimately hit this milestone at age 43. While I may not have done it in the time I had hoped, the reality was that it was done at a much larger, more complex company (Fortune 10). And while it took a little longer than I expected, the mental reframing kept me on course by remembering why I was doing this – legacy *and* impact.

The third and final concept is establishing how you will integrate your work and life priorities. It is impossible to do it all, but grounding to what matters most and to your path allows for your best to shine through. I remember a specific instance where I was given the opportunity to lead a 4-year, $65 million project that would span across the globe and would deliver major impact to the business unit, if successful. The previous project lead had been struggling for six months without any progress. With all eyes on me, I was able to deliver the plan within the remaining six months of the fiscal year, receiving significant recognition for it. This success continued in the following years, ultimately achieving our goal of doubling the business in just three years. This accomplishment propelled my career and caught the attention of the CEO and other leaders.

However, the immense dedication I poured into the project took a toll on my well-being. I found myself sleeping in short spurts and even working from a hospital bed with pneumonia. It was during this time that I realized the importance of self-care and well-being. High performance is crucial, but it cannot be sustained without taking care of yourself, both physically and mentally. Companies today understand the significance of well-being and invest in creating an environment that fosters belonging and psychological safety. This includes prioritizing what matters most and promoting work-life integration.

As a young manager at a Fortune 50 company who was fresh out of the hospital, this point was driven home to me through an intimate conversation with the CEO, who took notice of me. Nervously, I sought his advice on the topic and his words ended up being more valuable than I anticipated. With such a huge role and all his responsibilities, I wanted to know how he – the CEO – always seemed to have it all together. I shared my struggles with balancing work, family, and other responsibilities with him. His candid suggestion: prioritize what's most important and then treat these commitments with equal importance – never letting less impactful activities take you off course. In other words, anchor your why and your motivation to the notion that you cannot have impact, if you aren't in a healthy physical, mental and spiritual state.

This advice removed all the guilt that comes with trying to be everything to everyone, and his perspective helped me find a better work-life integration with those who matter most rather than striving for perfection and exact balance to everyone and everything. In part, my career skyrocketed, and it was a significant turning point and a valuable lesson that allowed me to be more authentic and impactful. Getting to your authentic state – truly being you – unlocks potential. When we realize how much energy is spent on trying to be something you are not or trying to do so much in areas that do not really drive *your* impact, we burn a lot of fuel without making it as far down the road as we'd like. Authenticity gives us the license to control the gas pedal, how you want it to be, versus how everyone else wants it from us.

So, you see, success, legacy, and leadership are all interconnected, and leaders must effectively embrace these concepts if to drive impact. None of us are perfect and we will fall from time to time. Our 'why' though will help us push through the obstacles to keep learning and progressing. Based on this perspective alone, I truly believe my family has made tremendous strides in our story and a remarkable shift from a mere two nickels to a leadership role at a Fortune 10 company. Combining these elements can be a powerful toolset in your own personal growth. And the reality is that it only takes one person to break generational cycles and create positive upward change; so why not be the one that can bring this outlook to your family. Let your story aid you in accomplishing your own goals.

CHAPTER 8

KEEPING THE FAITH

"Faith is the substance of things hoped for, the evidence of things not seen." - Hebrews 11:1

"I am not lucky, I am blessed."

-Carlos Quezada

Throughout my life doors have opened that I didn't even know existed. Opportunities have always come to me as if they came out of nowhere. I believe in the law of attraction, but I also know that my faith in God has also been the driving force of many blessings. Knowing that no matter what happens, I will always land on my feet because I'm being guided and protected by a higher power, gives me the strength and confidence I need to believe in my abilities.

As immigrants in this country, embarking on a journey to create a generational shift and achieve success is a daunting task. We're required to overcome numerous obstacles, such as learning a new language, adapting to cultural changes, and often being judged negatively, and misunderstood. However, it is crucial to recognize that there are limitations to our power in many situations. After we have done all, we can do, the rest is up to God.

In the face of adversity, it's imperative to maintain faith and trust in God. It's our faith that provides solace and strength when faced with obstacles that seem insurmountable. It reminds us that we are not alone in our journey and that there is a greater plan at work. When you believe in this with your whole heart, nothing can stop you.

DR. JOHNNY THOMAS

FAITH

By: Dr. Johnny Thomas

Working as an entrepreneur, administrator, and academic, I have been repeatedly reminded of the importance not only of particular choices and achievements but also, on a deeper level, of who I seek to be and become as a person. I want to share some of the key values that continue to inspire and energize me.

Since my time as an auditor—and before—I have been profoundly aware of the importance of *integrity*. That's a word different people use in different ways; what I mean when I use it here is a qualify of coherence, of internal and external consistency. I exhibit integrity when my life hangs together: when what I feel is manifest in what I say, when what I endorse in one dimension of my life is what is expressed elsewhere. Integrity is a quality that enables other people to rely one me—they know I'll be the same person from moment to moment, from setting to setting—and that equips me to count on myself, to know that I can be confident about how I'll react and what I'll do from day to day, from environment to environment. When I have integrity, I can make a coherent story out of my own life. That doesn't mean I can't grow and change; it does mean that I don't want to drift in response to this or that impulse or to respond to one situation differently than I would to another, relevantly similar, set of circumstances. Integrity means that, when I invest myself in a project, when I commit myself to a plan, I can count on myself to see it through, as can the others with whom I'm involved. And it means that others can trust what they see of me to reveal the real me.

It would have been hard not to learn the importance of *generosity* from my parents. Their dedication to the community in India where I grew up was palpable: the warmly supported people and institutions they cared about with their money, but also with their time and with their *presence*. Others knew that they would be there when it mattered. I've learned that opening my heart and my wallet and giving of my time to individual and causes can make a real difference.

Where we commit to being generous is one thing; but, once we do so, it's important to pay attention to ensuring that what we do exerts a meaningful *impact* on those we care about. When I give to people and projects, I seek to do so in a way that is realistically likely to be transformative. That means not giving just so I can feel I've done *something* but giving in a way that enables me to know I've done something *significant*. I care about being impactful because my goal isn't so much to feel good or to look good but to be and do good, and that means exhibiting the patience needed to ensure that how I attempt help will actually change things.

For as long as I can remember, I've treasured *relationships*. Connections with friends, family members, work colleagues, and participants in the lives of the various communities with which I'm affiliated are all inherently enriching, valuable for their own sake. I flourish in relationship, and relationships make me who I am, not just because they influence me but also because I understand myself as essentially connected—as a husband, father, son, friend, and so forth. Relationships teach me about who I am—I can see myself more clearly through other people's eyes—and about the world—since other people have experienced things I haven't. And relationships open up possibilities by extending my ability to influence the world and by opening doors for strategic alliances. I wouldn't be who I am without the relationships that help to constitute my identity.

Whether in the context of business, academia, or community engagement, *creativity* is crucial. Learning to look at problems in new ways, to generate and evaluate unexpected solutions is tool of immense practical value. And becoming a person who is willing to be destabilized and unsettled by what's novel is personally transformative. I don't want to be a person who's locked into a single way of seeing or doing things. Being creative liberates me from my own biases and limitations. Knowing the importance of creativity, I embrace it enthusiastically, along with the personal growth that accompanies it.

Over time, I've learned how important it is to exhibit *mercy*. It's crucial to avoid being judgmental, looking for opportunities to condemn, punishing. That's true because we probably wouldn't be willing to be subjected to other people's punitive attitudes, so we should avoid acting in light of those kinds of attitudes in relation to others. We need to see people as worth treasuring, asking not how we can pummel them into submission but how we can help and empower them. That doesn't mean that every person is right for every job or that every intimate relationship is safe; obviously not. But even when we have to say "no" to someone, we can do it without trying to punish, and we can look for ways of helping that person move forward on a worthwhile path. That's what each of us needs and deserves. I also find that, when I'm merciful, I let go of toxic emotions that get in the way of my own well being. Being a punisher doesn't make me a better person; but being merciful does.

Finally, I can't say enough about the importance of *gratitude*. Being grateful is a way of reminding myself and others that I didn't create my own life. I try to work diligently and creatively, but some things happen by accident and others occur because of the gifts I receive. Gratitude means both acknowledging the genuine value of those gifts and taking seriously the fact that they *are* gifts, rather than my own achievements. Being a grateful person is a way of understanding more clearly who I am in the world.

As you continue to grow as a person, give serious thought not just to what you do but who you are. When you do, I suspect you'll find that exhibiting integrity, generosity, sensitivity to impact, self-investment in relationships, creativity, mercy, and gratitude will enrich your life and the lives of the people you touch.

CHAPTER 9

THE GENERATIONAL SUCCESS STAIRCASE

"The immigrant success staircase is not just about individual accomplishments, but a collective narrative of resilience and adaptation."

- Unknown

In the rich tapestry of immigrant experiences, the narrative extends far beyond individual lifetimes, weaving a story of resilience, adaptation, and achievement across generations. The Immigrant Success Staircase aims to illuminate the unique progression of success within an immigrant family, tracing the path from the first daunting steps in a new land to the establishment of a lasting legacy of triumph.

First Generation - Navigating Uncharted Horizons

Our story begins with the pioneers, those courageous souls who boldly set foot on unfamiliar shores in search of opportunities and a better life. The first generation grapples with the intricacies of adapting to a new culture, overcoming language barriers, and laying the foundation for their family's future. In their pursuit, they often embark on humble beginnings, taking on entry-level jobs and immersing themselves in the challenges of assimilation.

Example:

Allow me to introduce you to Maria, a woman who arrived in the United States with a suitcase brimming with dreams. She toiled tirelessly in menial jobs, saving every hard-earned penny to provide a stable foundation for her family.

Second Generation - Navigating Dual Identities

Born in their adopted country, the second generation faces the unique challenge of balancing dual identities. They serve as the bridge between their cultural heritage and the society they call home. Education becomes a focal point, with aspirations for higher learning and professional growth.

Example:

Juan, Maria's son, dedicated himself to his studies throughout high school, becoming the first in the family to attend college. His success opened new doors and opportunities for the entire family.

Third Generation - Building Upon Achievements

The third generation, fully immersed in the culture, capitalizes on the groundwork laid by their predecessors. Education and professional success take center stage, with an increasing emphasis on contributing to the broader community. Entrepreneurship becomes a viable avenue, and the family's narrative begins to shift from overcoming challenges to achieving significant milestones.

Example:

Sofia, Juan's daughter, graduates with honors, enters a prestigious profession, and actively engages in community initiatives, embodying the family's upward trajectory.

Fourth Generation and Beyond: A Legacy of Success

Established in the United States, subsequent generations leverage the solid foundation laid by their forebears to further their success. Holding leadership roles, contributing to community development, and passing on the values of hard work and determination become defining features. The family's story transforms into a narrative of accomplishment and contribution.

Example:

Eduardo, Sofia's son, not only achieves professional success but also takes on the role of a mentor, guiding younger family members and actively participating in educational and community initiatives, ensuring the family legacy endures.

The success progression of an immigrant family across generations is a testament to the enduring spirit of perseverance, adaptation, and resilience. This journey reflects not only individual accomplishments but also a collective narrative of triumph over adversity. As each generation builds upon the achievements of the last, the family's story becomes a beacon of inspiration for others navigating the complex landscape of immigration and success. Every family's staircase is unique, filled with twists and turns, and may include setbacks. The purpose of this book is to empower and accelerate our immigrant community's journey towards reaching the pinnacle of the staircase while bridging generational gaps.

ABOUT THE AUTHOR

CARLOS QUEZADA

VP of Customer Experience
and Digital Engagement Strategy

Carlos Quezada

Carlos Quezada, a trailblazing Latino executive, currently serves as the Vice President of Customer Experience and Digital Engagement for a leading global Fortune 100 tech company. With an impressive 25-year career in the tech industry, Carlos has defied norms and earned recognition as one of the top 100 most influential Latinos in tech for three consecutive years. Hailing from Degollado, Jalisco, Mexico, Carlos immigrated to the U.S. at 14, embarking on an unconventional journey to reach the pinnacle of corporate success. Driven by gratitude, he sees it as his purpose to empower fellow Latinos and immigrants, actively engaging in community initiatives to inspire, educate, and foster success.

Made in the USA
Middletown, DE
20 May 2024